Managing Investor Relations

Managing Investor Relations

Strategies for Effective Communication

Alexander Laskin

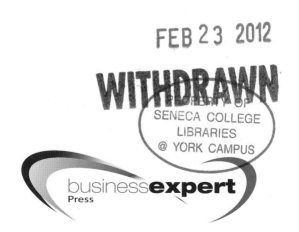

business**expert**
Press

Managing Investor Relations: Strategies for Effective Communication
Copyright © Business Expert Press, LLC, 2010.

First published in 2010 by
Business Expert Press, LLC
222 East 46th Street, New York, NY 10017
www.businessexpertpress.com

ISBN-13: 978-1-60649-080-8 (paperback)
ISBN-10: 1-60649-080-x (paperback)

ISBN-13: 978-1-60649-081-5 (e-book)
ISBN-10: 1-60649-081-8 (e-book)

DOI 10.4128/9781606490815

A publication in the Business Expert Press Corporate Communications collection

Collection ISSN: Forthcoming (print)
Collection ISSN: Forthcoming (electronic)

Cover design by Jonathan Pennell
Interior design by Scribe, Inc.

First edition: May 2010

10 9 8 7 6 5 4 3 2 1

Printed in Taiwan

Abstract

This book gives you an introduction to investor relations. Despite being a very young profession, investor relations today is widely recognized as one of the most important corporate communication functions. Whether you are a student considering employment in investor relations, a professional considering a career change to investor relations, or an investor relations officer looking for ways to improve performance, this book will provide you with answers to your questions.

First, the book discusses what investor relations is. Second, the book looks at the environment in which investor relations operates: the history of the profession, laws and regulations that govern the practice, and professional and ethical obligations of the investor relations officers. Third, the book describes the job functions of investor relations: from day-to-day tactical activities to big-picture strategies. Finally, the book suggests what the future of investor relations will look like and how it will affect the investor relations officers of tomorrow.

Keywords

Investor, shareholder, financial communications, corporate communications

Contents

CHAPTER 1

Introduction

This book is dedicated to one of the most important functions of modern corporations, investor relations. Investor relations is responsible for raising shareholder capital to enable corporations to implement their vision into reality. Investor relations helps companies survive through various stages of their development by enabling access to shareholder capital. Finally, investor relations ensures corporate executives are doing everything they can to lead corporations to long-term sustainable growth, while simultaneously benefiting the society and providing financial returns to shareholders.

The book consists of four sections. The first section discusses what investor relations is. The definition of the investor relations profession is discussed in detail, and key assumptions on which investor relations relies upon are analyzed.

The second section of the book includes chapters 3, 4, and 5 and is dedicated to the factors that influence the profession of investor relations. This section starts with the historic developments of the profession—changes in the societal and political environments created the need for investor relations and continued changing the functions and roles of investor relations professionals. Three periods in investor relations development are identified and described: *communication era*, *financial era*, and at present, *synergy era*. The historical changes and current state of legislature governing investor relations also are analyzed. The second section of the book concludes with the discussion of professional and ethical obligations of investor relations officers.

The third section of the book reviews the activities investor relations officers perform on day-by-day basis. Conference calls, investor meetings, annual reports, and other tactics that form the foundation of investor relations are discussed. From tactics, the book shifts to strategies. What is the strategic goal of investor relations? The book finds the answer in building relationships with the financial community to create *shareowners* out of *shareholders* with extended holding periods, active involvement with the company, and two-way communication with the corporate executives. The relationship building function of investor relations is analyzed and necessary components to the success of relationship building strategies—such as extended disclosure going beyond minimum financial disclosure requirements as well as increased focus on nonfinancial information that can explain the company's business model and future growth potential—are discussed. This section includes chapters 7, 8, 9, and 10.

Finally, the last section of the book tries to take a peek into the future of the profession. What will happen with investor relations tomorrow? How will the profession and professionals need to change to better adjust to the future demands that investors, legislators, and various financial market players impose on them? What will the continued globalization of the financial markets bring to the profession? How can the profession use to its best advantage the changing technological landscape with advent and adoption of electronic communications, social media, and instantaneous trades?

CHAPTER 2

What Is Investor Relations?

The professional organization of investor relations officers, National Investor Relations Institute (NIRI), adopted the latest definition of the profession in March 2003. Investor relations is defined as "a strategic management responsibility that integrates finance, communication, marketing and securities law compliance to enable the most effective two-way communication between a company, the financial community, and other constituencies, which ultimately contributes to a company's securities achieving fair valuation."[1] This definition was a significant step forward from the previous version adopted by NIRI in 1996, where investor relations was labeled "a marketing activity" with the purpose of "providing an accurate portrayal of a company" in order to have "a positive effect on a company's value."

The current definition moves away from the narrow marketing focus on sales and promotions as it now includes finance, communications, and law to the mix of investor relations activities. This is indicative of the changes that the field of investor relations experienced at the start of the 21st century with the wave of corporate scandals and changes in securities regulations (described later in chapter 5). Indeed, today investor relations cannot be a simple marketing activity—rather, it is a strategic management responsibility. Investor relations is not concentrated within the investor relations department—the whole company is run with the interests of shareholders in mind. Investor relations officers must be members of the top management team and be present whenever key corporate decisions are being made rather than simply communicate, or market, these decisions to shareholders after they have been decided upon. The investor relations officer's responsibility is to make sure the interests of investors and shareholders are taken into account and, in the event they are not, raise this issue in front of all corporate managers and the board of directors to ensure that decisions that do not meet the interests of shareholders are not accepted.

Another important change in the definition was the addition of two-way communications. Two-way communications was added to the definition of investor relations to substitute one-way flow of providing information about the company. Previously, investor relations was often equated with disclosure—we put information out there, the rest is not our business. The shareholders, however, demanded to be heard. The feedback loop in communications is a necessity. As the influence of shareholders grows, the companies that refuse to listen to shareholders suffer.

In fact, companies should demand from their investor relations officers to conduct shareholder research in order to learn who owns the stock, why they own the stock, and what shareholders think about the company, its management, and the decisions that management makes. NIRI recommends, "The company's investor relations officer . . . should be required to meet with an independent committee of the board . . . to report feedback from investors and analysts."[2]

The feedback is analyzed at the highest level of the organizational hierarchy and is used in the decision making and strategic planning. CEOs expect their investor relations officers to be actively engaged in the corporate decision making and supply the information from shareholders and about shareholders to the management team. Indeed, it is vital for the management of the company to know who the organization's investors are as such knowledge enables the company to serve investors better. Kevin Rollins, former president of Dell Inc., explains, "We've also charged our investor relations team with sharing and interpreting feedback from the investment community for us . . . ultimately, my job and Michael's [CEO Michael Dell] job is to lead Dell in a way that drives sustainable, dependable shareholder value over time."[3]

The third important change in the definition concerned the overall goal of the investor relations activities. Earlier, the goal was to have a positive effect on the share price—the higher the better. Enron's disaster can arguably be attributed to such a view on investor relations. Current definition of investor relations emphasizes the need for a "fair value" as opposed to a "high value." The goal is to help investors and financial analysts understand the true value of the company's business and to help them adjust their estimates no matter if it means decrease or increase in the stock price. In other words, mistaken overevaluation can be as dangerous for the company as underevaluation as it can be a source of sudden volatility in stock price and trading volume. Effective investor relations becomes the foundation of the capital markets that depend on the complete and timely disclosure of relevant information. Investor relations cannot hide any information, either positive or negative, as it will lead to mistakes in the evaluation of the company's stock.

Investor relations practiced in the way described above—integrated into the top management decisions process, based on two-way communications, and aiming for a fair stock valuation—can become a source of competitive advantage for a corporation. And this competitive advantage is quite important. Indeed, companies are accustomed to competing on the product markets. Companies producing TV sets know other producers of TV sets, their product lineups, price points, major production facilities, and technological innovations. The competition is typically contained within one industry, and it is quite possible to track the changing landscape of this particular industry. Investor relations, on the other hand, is responsible for competition for capital. This competition is not limited to any particular industry. In fact, a company on the capital markets competes with any other publicly traded company from various industries and from all over the globe. This competition is extremely complex and tracking this changing environment is an enormous task.

Yet the shareholder capital is a scarce resource, and not every business can get access to the financial resources. So if a company needs capital to finance growth or enter new markets or simply needs resources beyond its cash flow, it becomes a job of the investor relations departments to identify investors for the company, target them with company's communications, create opportunities for the investors to acquire stock in the company, and establish and maintain relationships with them.

It is a constant effort—it is not sufficient to attract investors and then abandon any communications with them. Investors have an opportunity to sell the company's stock. One also cannot rely just on its performance—actions do not always speak for themselves. Marcus and Wallace compare investor relations with a hoop: "It keeps rolling only as long as you keep hitting it with a stick. The minute you stop, the hoop stops and falls over."[4]

The modern concept of investor relations is part of the efficient market hypothesis. The efficient market hypothesis assumes that all markets are in equilibrium: all securities are fairly priced, and all provide equal returns. In this situation, no investor can consistently beat the market, and thus there is no reason to constantly buy and sell shares of companies trying to outperform the average market return.

The efficient market hypothesis, however, requires key assumptions to be met: all relevant information about the company and its performance is publicly available, all market participants have equal access to such information on a timely basis, and all investors are rational and capable of evaluating the information available to them. Investor relations is charged with providing the information from the company to shareholders, financial analysts, and other market participants.

In this situation, investor relations becomes a key activity not just for a particular company but for the whole modern economy. The survival of modern capitalism depends on how well investor relations officers perform their task in ensuring equal access to information for various financial market participants. Thus, investor relations is charged with the task of ensuring that the key assumptions of the efficient market hypothesis are met through extensive and timely disclosure of all relevant information pertaining to the company and its stock.

CHAPTER 3

Investor Relations: Past

The history of the investor relations profession is not very long. It is a young specialization that is still forming today. Yet it is possible to recognize two separate periods in the historic development of investor relations in the United States: the communication era and the financial era. The beginning of the *communication era* can generally be dated back to 1945, while the start of the *financial era* dates back to 1975. The present era of investor relations, synergy era, started in 2002.

Communication Era

The earliest mention of the investor relations function can be traced back to Ralth Cordiner, a chairman of General Electric, who in 1953 created a department in charge of all shareholder communications.[1] In the late 1950s and 1960s, investor relations departments started appearing at a number of large companies; consulting agencies first began offering investor relations services. Most of the investor relations work, however, focused on putting the word about organizations out and on attracting attention of financial publics to the stock. David Silver recalls that "investor relations emerged into its own in the 1960s, often associated . . . with the so-called dog and pony shows for sell-side analysts and retail investors, usually held at the offices of securities brokerages."[2]

The development of the investor relations profession was a response to the changing economic and sociopolitical environments. The economic boom of the 1950s generated wealth for private Americans and, at the same time, encouraged business expansion to satisfy the constantly growing needs of consumers. The corporations needed money to grow and develop; people needed a way to invest surplus income. In this situation, the meeting of the two worlds was inevitable. DeWitt Morrill reminisces,

The public, for the first time, began to get into the market. True, individuals had played the market in the 1920s, but nothing to match the numbers and trading volume of the 1950s and 1960s. Where the markets of pre-Depression era were financed largely by credit (no margin requirements!), sad memories and new laws governing securities markets stirred post-WWII investors to favor cash. It is not surprising that this confluence of forces found expression in rising stock prices. Corporate earnings rose strongly—but price-earning multiples expanded even more. The circumstances were made-to-order for successful investing, no matter how speculative it was inherently. The rising tide was lifting all boats.[3]

The new kind of player on the financial market—a private shareholder—caused some changes in the boardrooms across the country. The consumer-product corporations realized first that these new shareholders were also fruitful targets for consumer marketing efforts. And vice versa, consumers of the company's products could be targeted to become shareholders. The first corporations to strategically target private shareholders-consumers were car companies such as Ford, GM, and Chrysler. Indeed, shareholders were likely to purchase a car made by the company in which they owned stock rather than made by its competitor. Increasing the demand for stock became an important part of the corporate agenda: "Occupants of the executive suites were quick to see, that all of this demand for stock was helping to push prices up and up. This helped immensely to finance growth, enhance empires."[4]

The companies accustomed to competing on the product markets brought similar tactics, resources, and budgets to their competition on the financial markets. It is not a surprise then that in this situation management turned to the recognized experts who were already engaged with the consumers—advertisement and public relations. Investor relations became viewed as an extension of public relations function.

In the 1950s, however, public relations was not a well-established practice itself. Only the largest companies had internal public relations staff, and the functions and roles of public relations were quite limited. At that time, public relations was still struggling for the right to strategically manage itself as it was often a purely technical function of media relations. Public relations education and research were not fully developed. Lack of a systematized body of knowledge and qualified educated personnel made it difficult for public relations to provide quality service in the investor relations field. Although pioneers of public relations, having acquired tremendous experience during World War II, started offering strategic counseling, for many public relations was still mere press-agentry: "The practitioners in the field, along with the whole discipline of public relations itself, just 'grew like Topsy' without a common body of knowledge or without evolving any theory to guide their problem-solving efforts."[5]

As a result, the new and not-well-established public relations function was suddenly charged with the additional duties of investor relations—a job for which most practitioners on the corporate or agency sides were not qualified. So, they approached this new task in the same way they performed their public relations tasks—relying on press-agentry and publicity. Morrill reminisces that investor relations in these early years was "transformed into publicity, promotion and pageants." He provides several examples of investor relations in the 1950s era:

- The annual reports suddenly blossomed as a 48-page, glossy sales brochure for the company's products. The financial were there, mandatorily, but the sell was in the sizzle, not the steak.
- The annual meeting became a huge, free-for-all gala. A large eastern railroad put together a special train for stockholders and carried them first class to a company-owned hotel in the southern Appalachians for the meeting.
- An international telecommunications company held a large gathering under two large tents in central New Jersey. A bountiful lunch was served, and there were several open bars. Members of the press were delivered in limousines from New York and returned the same way. Products were richly displayed. The chairman, himself a noted gourmet and bon vivant, addressed the gathering. Reactions were enthusiastic—but absolutely nothing of substance was done.
- Companies made gifts or gift boxes of products available to shareholders, sometimes free. Liquor companies also provided their products under advantageous purchase agreements.[6]

Investor relations largely practiced as financial press-agentry and publicity, however, often satisfied the interests of many private shareholders who lacked understanding of finance and business in general. Even more importantly, such investor relations practices often satisfied many corporate executives who were not ready to share their powers with shareholders.

Indeed, the variety of new private shareholders was a new experience for many corporations in the 1950s and created another incentive (along with the need to compete for capital) for the formation of the investor relations departments. In fact, before World War II there were just a few wealthy stockholders who did not pay much attention to the company's management, did not attend annual meetings, and never complained. The new owners, however, were quite different. First of all, there were a lot of them, and they were constantly growing in numbers. They owned very small amount of stock. Yet they had a strong sense of ownership. All these new shareholders constantly demanded more information and attention from the corporations: they wanted a steady stream of information; they wanted all the details; they wanted to meet with the top executives; and they wanted good news as well as bad news.

These were different types of publics Wall Street had to get used to:

> At the outset of the Bull market, a large chunk of the new money going into stocks came from those WWII-time savers who had little to spend their war industry wages on. These were not youth fresh from the field of the battle, but many who had suffered through the Depression and the cataclysmic closing of the banks in 1932. They were determined to keep a close eye on the funds they had entrusted to management and the stock markets, neither of which they really trusted.[7]

These new shareholders craved information, yet because of their large numbers, it was difficult to communicate with all of them directly. The financial intermediaries who transmit large amounts of financial information today were not well developed in the 1950s—most shares were owned directly by private shareholders.

These shareholders actively demanded communications, and the management needed to communicate with this group. At the same time, the management did not take the private shareholders seriously. First of all, managers were used to being the ones who ran the show—and they were not intending to change that. Second, there were other ways of acquiring capital such as banks and insurance companies. Finally, executives could not justify meeting the demands of uneducated shareholders with a couple of shares—it did not seem that shareholders can have any real power.

At the same time, corporate executives started feeling a certain threat to the status quo from these new shareholders. So, top managers were looking for a way to communicate with these shareholders from a distance, to give them information without meeting with them in person, preferably without any chance for shareholders to respond or ask questions. In addition, these communications should not have required many efforts or resources. Here enters media relations again!

Today, hardly anyone would equate investor relations with media relations. Laskin claims that media relations is among the lowest priority tasks for today's investor relations officers.[8] In the 1950s, however, great attention of investor relations practitioners and agencies focused on the mass media, namely the press.

All these caused problems for investor relations—shareholders invested their own money and wanted attention from the corporations: they needed to discuss the company's prospects for future growth instead of receiving gift baskets. Shareholders were interested in meeting with the chief executive officer (CEO) or chief financial officer (CFO) of the company—people who know the strategy and the operations of company—and instead had to communicate through a newspaper. The role of financial analysts was simply ignored. Finally, people in charge of public relations and suddenly in charge of investor relations did not understand accounting or financial analysis and often had very limited mathematical skills. Public relations was set up to fail in investor relations—it just came too early.

The new investor relations profession was looking for people who could understand the financials and at the same could produce required communication tactics, but such people were rare exceptions. The public relations practitioners were not trained to handle the financial markets:

Punctilious attention to financial details was not one of their strong units. The story was. They were skilled in using the media, and the brokerage community, to propagate stories about their clients best calculated to arouse investor attention. Often they did not really understand more than the bare rudiments of what they were trying to sell. . . . The trend to producing, peddling and promoting half-truths and untruths, even if cloaked in hedged language, was increasing at an accelerating rate—a sort of monkey see, monkey do syndrome.[9]

In addition, the corporations did not have any interest in listening to their shareholders—the focus was on a one-way stream of information from the company to the financial publics. Chatlos, the founder and former President of NIRI, notes, "The trickle of information sponsored by corporations became a torrent."[10] Companies tried to drown investors in all the data poured on them. Yet no feedback was collected or analyzed.

Publicity and press-agentry tactics contributed substantially to development of many negative connotations that the term *public relations* has today. This was also the cause for the term *investor relations* to acquire negative connotations. Later, the investor relations profession engaged in significant efforts to actively distinguish itself from public relations and disassociate from public relations education, professional association, and consulting agencies. Cutlip, Center, and Broom observe,

As press agents grew in number and their exploits became more outrageous—albeit successful, more often than not—it was natural that they would arouse the hostility and suspicion of editors and inevitable that the practice and its practitioners would become tainted. This stigma remains as part of the heritage of public relations.[11]

The same stigma tainted public relations in the financial world. Financial publics lost credibility in public relations practitioners, their ethics, integrity, or simply capabilities of handling investor relations. Investor relations engaged in significant efforts to distinguish itself from any public relations background. If initially joining Public Relations Society of America (PRSA) was considered, in the 1960s investor relations practitioners began talks about the need to create their own professional organization.

The investor relations practitioners cited several problems in joining PRSA, such as differences regarding the name of the specialization, ethical standards and enforcement, and professional development in special skills. In the minds of those active in early efforts to organize the field of investor relations, public relations was synonymous with publicists, who promoted rather than informed and relied on persuasion, manipulation, and deception. "In the investor relations view, financial public relations was a glaring oxymoron."[12]

At the end of this first era of investor relations evolution, two professions, investor relations and public relations, split completely. Investor relations practitioners formed their own association and proclaimed that public relations "chaff" would not be allowed to join. The association, first named Investor Relations Association (IRA), later changed its name to the National Investor Relations Institute (NIRI). One of the first documents of the organization declares its main goal: "Our aim is to separate ourselves from the so-called financial public relations consultants, who operate on the fringe of stock touting, and who are fouling the nest."[13] The association adopted a practice to conduct background checks on applicants and engaged in several other activities to protect itself from public relations practitioners.

As a result of this history, the investor relations profession in its early years was heavily dominated by publicity and press-agentry. This created a bad stigma for any public relations or communication professionals in the area of investor relations. The end of this period is associated with the dissatisfaction by shareholders and financial intermediaries with such investor relations practices. The profession of investor relations had to start rebuilding its tainted image by actively disassociating itself from public relations. Finally, investor relations officers left public relations professional associations to create their own association, NIRI. The association engaged in background checks to keep public relations out. The pendulum was swinging the other way too fast—much of the valid communication and public relations expertise became voluntarily cut off and disregarded as unnecessary for the investor relations profession.

Financial Era

Changes in the economy once again brought changes to the profession of investor relations. The 1970s saw the shift from individual retail investors to institutional investors.

On one side, the enormous growth of investment activities in the 1950s and 1960s put pressure on the financial markets infrastructure. As mentioned earlier, the growth in individual investments was exponential in the years after World War II. The number of individual shareholders increased from 4.5 million in 1952 to over 20 million in 1965, which represents every sixth adult in the United States. Chatlos reminisces,

> As the trading and brokerage system creaked and strained under the increasing load of activity imposed on it, Wall Street's response was less than prudent. Profitable success after success as "the only game in town" proved to be a harsh taskmaster to the system. When problems emerged because sale activities were extended beyond the back offices' ability to handle the resulting volume, the immediate response was arrogant quick fixes rather than anticipatory long-term business planning.[14]

Banks stopped taking on any new clients. Brokers became peculiar in choosing who to work with or whom to drop from the client list. The processing times were long, and the services were not friendly.

Another problem was the track record. The market was growing in leaps and bounds after World War II, and shareholders (especially individual shareholders) expected it to continue like this forever. Morrill paints a colorful picture:

> It was an era of tips. You could get advice from the taxi driver, the waiter, the barber, the shoe shine man who came through the office to keep the gloss intact. Cocktail parties, subway trains and airport clubs all sported a lively conversation about the market. People on a wide scale had reached the point where they believed that all trees grow to the sky, and the market will always go up.[15]

The expectations became too high for the reality to deliver. The financial markets were destroying themselves: the system built on volume of transactions could not handle that volume anymore, and the customers were ready to quit. Chatlos concludes,

> Customers were less than happy and did what might have been expected. They walked away. They did not sell their shares. They just walked away. For a system geared to the retail trade—and in many respects it remains so today—it was a devastating blow. The system was geared to volume, couldn't plan for high volume, and suddenly had very little volume. Again, as could have been expected, broker failures and bankruptcy-avoiding mergers followed. It was a grim sight and the individual shareholder moved further away from the system.[16]

The stock market had to institutionalize. It became necessary to consolidate millions of private shareholders into smaller number of professional institutional investors. This, however, meant a very different crowd at shareholder meetings—instead of poorly educated private shareholders the meetings became dominated by overqualified financial analysts. Indeed, "because of the legal fiduciary responsibilities to their clients, these institutions have demanded detailed and timely strategic and financial information."[17] Financial analysts could not be satisfied by glossy annual reports and gift baskets—they needed information on the company strategy, sales, and research and development.

In addition, financial analysts themselves were not accustomed to dealing with investor relations officers. In fact, analysts were around even before the 1970s but in the previous communication era they did not communicate with the investor relations departments. Investor relations officers were mostly occupied with the retail shareholders, the dominant market force of the time. The job of communicating with analysts from the earliest times was assigned to a CFO or an accountant. As a result, when the 1970s brought the shift from retail to institutional ownership, many of institutional analysts already had their preestablished contacts at the organization—most often in the finance department or treasury. Even more, many of analysts were not even aware that they needed to communicate with the investor relations officer. They tended to go to the same source they used to go to earlier—a person in the treasury or finance department.

Investor relations previously geared toward private retail shareholder was becoming less and less relevant. The target audience of investor relations was changing, and the profession was not sure how to handle it. Instead of less than knowledgeable private shareholders, overqualified stock analysts and institutional investors became the main contacts for the investor relations. The role of mass media communications in investor relations suddenly lost its importance. Public relations practitioners were losing the grip on investor relations, while the financial departments were engaging in talks with analysts and institutional investors more and more often.

Most CEOs, however, were actively trying to avoid the financial gurus of Wall Street as much as they had been trying to avoid private shareholders earlier. Executives were used to being the ones running the show, and they did not plan on sharing their powers with either poorly educated private shareholders or overeducated financial analysts. However, private shareholders were easy to deal with and could be kept at bay by using mass media and giving them occasional handouts.

Financial analysts, on the other hand, presented a larger problem. They were not satisfied by the little amount of substantial information the companies were disclosing. They asked questions, sometimes questions "that management had not asked itself, or for various reasons did not want to answer."[18] Even more, they had power over the companies they owned stock in and perhaps even more power over the companies they did not invest in. A large institutional player could sweep all the company's shares off the market, pushing the price up just to unload them all several days later plummeting the stock.

> The new institutions had so much money to invest that there literally was not enough time to observe the prudent ground rules. The new method was to dump the shares when a sell decision was made and to buy as quickly as possible when that decision was made. This had a severe impact on market price volatility.[19]

If earlier private shareholders at least smoothed out this volatility, in the 1970s with individuals off the market, the price was in the hands of the financial analysts. A single word the executive said might have changed the price of stock enormously.

The management decided they would rather avoid meeting with analysts altogether for the fear of saying something wrong, choosing instead to forward the calls to the CFO or treasury departments. Dissatisfied with the way investor relations professionals treated them, financial analysts were happy to talk with the CFO. In addition, financial analysts felt that CFO is better qualified and more knowledgeable about the company than an investor relations professional. Over time, the responsibilities for investor relations shifted to CFOs and treasury departments. It is not a surprise that when CFOs were hiring to fill an investor relations vacancy, they often looked for financial or accounting backgrounds. Management often saw former financial analysts to be ideal investor relations officers because they were expected to easily find a common language with the other financial analysts and professional investors.

As a result, the role of the investor relations professional was also evolving. Powerful and knowledgeable institutional investors evaluated every action the company took and were not afraid to ask questions and criticize if they did not believe the action was in the best interests of shareholders. The new institutional investors were the corporate activists:

> They have successfully sought an activist role in corporate governance, focusing their institutional power on company's performance, the proper role of the board of directors, and executive compensation. . . . The overall impact of the institutionalization of U.S. equity markets has been to make the job of the investor relations executive infinitely more challenging and complex.[20]

Investor relations professionals had to transform from provider of information into defenders of managers' decisions—if investors had critique for company actions, investor relations were expected to provide counterarguments to explain and protect the company actions. Proactive investor relations practices called for anticipating shareholders' reactions and preparing to respond to them in advance. Shareholder research became a necessity. Other investor relations officers simply did not allow negative questions to be asked at conferences and annual meetings, tightly controlling the communication channels. It became a common practice in preparation for conference calls to create lists of names that operators should not allow to ask questions.

The focus of the investor relations profession shifted to persuasion and making the sell. Investor relations became "the process by which we inform and persuade investors of the value inherent in the securities we offer as means to capitalize business."[21] More and more financial analysts started becoming investor relations officers and consultants and shifted the role of the profession to help the management "to package their story for institutional buyers or sell-side analysts."[22]

This financial era of investor relations history was focused on professional investors and financial analysts. For the tasks of defending the corporation in front of them, CEOs and CFOs were hiring former financial analysts who became the new investor relations professionals. They lacked public relations knowledge and skills, but they understood the numbers and knew the rules of Wall Street. Executives decided that it was good enough, and they were quite happy to have these new employees between themselves and the professional investment community. The role of investor relations was to increase the valuation of the company—the good information was widely distributed and the bad news was tightly controlled. The communication was manipulated to put a positive spin on every action of the company. The results of these changes in investor relations became visible in overvaluations, accounting fraud, and selective distribution of information.

CHAPTER 4

Investor Relations: Present

Today the role and scope of investor relations are undergoing more changes. Protecting the company and its management through persuasion and advocacy gives way to dialogue and development of long-term understanding. As with the previous eras, the shift to the current era in the development of investor relations, *synergy era*, was caused by changes in the economy and society.

The shocking corporate failures of the early 21st century, including the collapse of dot-coms and accounting scandals at the largest companies, put the whole model of the corporate America to the test. Indeed, scandals with financial accounting practices at Enron, Tyco, Global Crossings, Williams, and other corporations called for more scrutiny of disclosure standards and investor relations in general. Laskin suggests that the collapse of Enron was the wake-up call for investor relations practice that now has to assume more responsibilities than ever before.[1]

Suddenly, the unprecedented growth in the stock market was replaced by recession. The competition for capital became more intense. Investor relations became one of the key activities that could make or break a corporation; CEOs saw that investor relations is not one of the auxiliary functions, but an activity that can create a competitive advantage.[2]

The scandals led to stiffer regulations from the Securities and Exchange Commission (SEC) and Congress with the passage of the Sarbanes-Oxley Act in 2002, which was aimed at improving corporate governance and making managers and boards of directors more accountable. The Act expanded the scope of required disclosures and changed the disclosure procedures. But despite the expanded disclosure, investor relations today has to go beyond publications of obligatory disclosure documents. Investor relations is not about the amount of information provided. Rather, it is about understanding. Investor relations' task is to help investors understand the company and its business model. The goal is not to have as high a valuation as possible but rather a fair value of the stock price. Finding the right investors, building trust and relationships with them, and developing long-term ownership patterns to combat volatility are the new goals for the professionals.[3]

Investors themselves are changing. They are not satisfied with information in the obligatory disclosure filings despite the increased amount of such information. They want to know the company's strategy, management team, its vision, and role in the society. Today, communications targeted at investors "have to be able to explain not only the numbers, but also the nature of the business, its long-term strategy, and non-financial information, as investors have learned to incorporate these higher-level questions into their buy and sell decisions."[4]

The long-known equation return on equity (ROE) is being transformed into return on expectations, and managing these expectations becomes an important part of investor relations programs:

> Prevailing wisdom is that inasmuch as it [investor relations] deals largely with financial data it is best left in the Financial Department and, perhaps, staffed by ex-security analysts, lawyers or others comfortable with numbers. . . . This may be yesterday's rationale. The ROE analysts are really interested in Return on Expectations. We submit that too often missing from the "quants" communications is any sense of corporate vision; or long range strategic rationale; or corporate competence; or leadership—all subjective values better left to broad-gauged PR [public relations] people to communicate.[5]

Although it is doubtful that public relations professionals will be much better at investor relations than ex-financial analysts, the importance of communicating both "quants" and "quals" cannot be doubted. Thus, perhaps, instead of arguing that investor relations is better left to communication specialists as was the case in the earliest era of investor relations history or that investor relations is better left to financial specialists as was the case in the second era, the profession can start working on integrating both areas of expertise. And as such enters the third (*synergy*) era of investor relations development.

Today's investor relations cannot suffice with only financial disclosure—investors are not interested in seeing 10-Q or 10-K. Rather, investors are interested in understanding the company, its business model, and its value-generation capabilities. If it involves reading a 10-K, investors will read it. But typically it requires more than that. This is exactly where investor relations can earn its mark—helping investors understand the company. In turn, it means that "the communication skills of the IR specialists will be more important than ever."[6] It becomes important for investor relations officers not only to be able to know the words of the investor relations language (financial terms) but also to know the grammar of this language and the proper ways to use these words (strategic communication). In other words, both areas of expertise, business and communication, are essential to the modern practice of investor relations.

The changes in the media landscape and communication technologies also brought changes to investor relations. Today one can hardly isolate messages intended for shareholders from messages intended for consumers—access to media channels and instantaneous widespread communication technologies make information a commodity. From the information age, when information was the most treasured asset, we are now in the postinformation age, when information is widely available to everybody and in fact commoditized. Communication professionals can hardly limit their messages to a specific geographic region, demographic group, or type of public. Employees, investors, consumers, suppliers, and others can easily gain access to the messages intended for other types of publics.

As a result, investor relations officers might take into account the impact of investor relations messages not just on investors but also on employees, consumers, and others. People who represent their companies today must "possess extraordinary public relations skills and understand the implications of upcoming announcements for all of the company's major stakeholders—including employees and the community—and not just the shareholders."[7] In this environment, integration of all communication functions, such as investor relations, public relations, marketing, community relations and similar, under one umbrella can create a competitive advantage for a corporation. David Silver goes further saying that "the convergence of IR and PR has become so important that not combining those functions could have negative consequences for a public company's share price."[8]

This shift demands a return of communication expertise back into the investor relations profession. In fact, today's investor relations requires expertise in both areas—communication and finance—to be present and coexist. Such investor relations practice will finally be what pioneers of investor relations envisioned as communication and finance merger to create sophisticated and successful investor relations programs. Investor relations officers will need to gain proficiency in both areas as well through dual degrees, graduate degrees, or professional training.

A *Harvard Business Review* article discusses the need for this new era of synergy:

> Aside from those companies that assign to the investor relations function whoever happens to be available (one major corporation, for example, gave investor relations duties to a retired chemist), many organizations make one of two common errors:
>
> 1. Some companies will decide that investor relations are properly a part of public relations. They are unaware that many security analysts feel uncomfortable when talking with public relations people because, rightly or wrongly, analysts are generally suspicious of being "snowed."
>
> 2. Other companies assume that the best candidate for the investor relations function is found in the treasurer's or controller's department. Security analysts, the reason, are figure-happy, and who is better qualified to throw around statistics than the man who has lived with them? Such reasoning is unsound, and if it accomplishes nothing else, it serves to demonstrate that the chief executive of the company has not got the message of what investor relations is all about. A moment's reflection will reveal that knowledge of the figure does not, per se, establish ability to communicate that knowledge effectively.
>
> The solution to be found lies somewhere between these two extremes. The best candidate for the investor relations post will have had experience in both public relations and the financial phases of a company's operations.[9]

The synergy era requires investor relations officers to be experts in both communications and finance, as well as to have knowledge about securities laws. The new investor relations professionals are not mere advocates of management—they listen to investors and analysts and bring the feedback to the company. The shareholder research and collection of feedback from the financial community becomes of vital importance. But it is not enough to passively listen to shareholders—proactive activities are required to encourage investors and analysts to share feedback with the company. Proactive activities are also required to learn about the companies' shareholders themselves: Why do they own the stock in the company? How long do they own the stock? Where did they acquire it, and under what conditions will they sell it? What other companies and industries do they own stock in? How would they like to receive information from the company? What other sources of information they rely upon? Investor relations officers must have programs in place that would ask and find answers to these and many other questions to make sure that company knows its shareholders and analysts following the company and knows them well.

This feedback serves both the management of the company and the shareholders. Investor relations facilitate the exchange of ideas between the management and the financial community. Shareholders should be as likely to persuade management to adopt the shareholders' propositions as management is likely to persuade the shareholders to follow management's recommendations. Similar to the two-way symmetrical communication model[10] or mixed-motive model,[11] investor relations professionals become loyal both to their employers and to the target publics. The goal of the investor relations is to have the interests of shareholders and managements aligned. Indeed, serving investors is the exact work that corporations' management requires from the investor relations officers. Lou Thompson, former president of NIRI, elucidates,

> The role of investor relations is to minimize investor risk by assuring that the company is providing information that is clear and understandable through means that achieve full and fair disclosure. The lower the perceived risk in investing in a company, the lower the company's cost of capital. There is a true bottom line benefit of full and fair disclosure.[12]

In other words, the more investor relations officers serve the public and the investment community, the better they serve the organization because it decreases investor's risk and thus decreases the cost of capital for the company. Two-way communications appear to be at the very heart of the investor relations profession.

In addition, in today's investment market, the responsibilities of investor relations officers to the investment community are growing at large. Investor relations must become pioneers in efforts to change the rules of financial disclosure or change other aspects of financial markets if they learn investors' dissatisfaction with the current practices. It is a job of investor relations officers to ensure the markets operate smoothly, providing companies with access to capitals and investors with understanding how that capital is being used.

The previous eras saw investor relations officers as technicians following management's directions or responding to shareholders' requests. Investor relations officers were mostly consumed by technical rather than strategic activities: "An exclusive emphasis on intended technical activities deflects attention from the symbolic nature of investor relations departments and the institutional sources of organizational structure."[13] Investor relations today, however, is becoming a management responsibility with certain autonomy and decision-making power within the corporate structure. Investor relations professionals are engaged in more proactive communications than before through meetings with analysts and investors, roadshows, conference participations, and so on.[14]

The modern *synergy* era of investor relations was caused by many changes in the economy, technology, regulations, increased shareholders' attention to the role of corporations in the society, and many other factors. These changes placed new demands on the investor relations professionals and required the investor relations function to adapt. "The methods of investor relations are continuing to undergo changes in the wake of scandals, revised government regulations and legislation, increased knowledge levels of investment community, new technology, the global investment marketplace, and overall societal desires for transparency and ethical business operation."[15] To respond to these challenges, investor relations has to combine the expertise of both communication and finance to devise sophisticated two-way symmetrical programs to facilitate dialogue between company's management and the financial community with the purpose of enhancing mutual understanding. Loss of investor confidence resulting from scandals, newly imposed regulatory requirements, and shareholder activism should be addressed by open and clear communications.[16]

Indeed, "success in investor relations requires the companies to extend the scope of investor relations from a mere publication of obligatory annual and interim reports to more frequent, extensive, proactive and diversified two-way interaction and communication."[17] Investor relations is not about numbers anymore; today's investor relations is about building and maintaining relationships. Investor relations officers must become proficient communicators with knowledge and skills of both public relations practitioner and financial analyst. Thus, the synergy era calls for integration of communication and financial components of investor relations. Investor relations officers in the synergy era have expertise in both finance and communication. Investor relations activities in the synergy era focus on long-term relationship building activities. Investor relations becomes a managerial proactive activity based on research to anticipate the relevant issue rather than a technical reactive function. Such investor relations is based on two-way symmetrical communications between the company and the financial community.

It is possible to conclude that the modern state of the investor relations profession is a direct result of the investor relations history. The profession of investor relations and investor relations professionals went through significant changes over the last 60 years or so. As described earlier, the first era of investor relations, the communication era, was characterized by the lack of financial expertise among investor relations practitioners. Investor relations tasks were assigned to publicists who were largely press agents and technicians focusing their job on putting the company's name into mass media. Investor relations in this period lacked strategic and managerial activities. The organizations did not conduct research to understand their shareholding patterns. The feedback from shareholders was not collected. It was a one-way stream of information: from organization to the investors, mostly through the mass media channels.

The second era, financial era, saw the shift of investor relations responsibilities from communication specialists to accountants and financial professionals. Under the supervision of CFOs, investor relations activities became focused on providing financial disclosure to investors.

The focus from mass media changed to one-on-one meetings with institutional shareholders and financial analysts. This changing nature of communications enabled two-way information streams. Feedback was gathered. It was, however, rarely used to modify the activities of corporations. Rather, it was used to craft more persuasive messages to "sell" the organization. The "selling" approach positioned the goal of investor relations in increasing the share price to maximize equity value: the higher the stock price the better. This might have been one of the reasons for the "creative accounting" at Enron and other corporations.

Currently, investor relations enters the third era, the synergy era. Both communication and financial skill-sets are valued equally high for their contribution to investor relations. The goal of the function is the improved understanding of the company among investors and analysts. Investor relations officers are looking for a fair value rather than high value—overvaluation is perhaps as bad as undervaluation. It is two-way communication with information traveling from organizations to investors and back from investors to organizations. Feedback from investors is actively sought, and shareholder research is conducted. The feedback is analyzed at the highest level of the organizational hierarchy and is used in the decision making and strategic planning. CEOs expect their investor relations officers to be actively engaged in the corporate decision making and supply the information from shareholders and about shareholders to the management team.

The focus of the synergy era on the improved understanding of the company requires investor relations to provide both positive and negative information. The goal is not high value of stock, but fair value of stock. To create better understanding of the corporate business value, companies have to expand their communications with shareholders from obligatory financial disclosure to include the information beyond U.S. generally accepted accounting principles (GAAP), the information "that supplements and complements a firm's financial statements."[18] More and more, the focus of investor meetings shifts to intangible and nonfinancial aspects of business. The Centre for the Management of Environmental and Social Responsibility explains, "Investors increasingly consider non-financial aspects in their assessment of companies."[19] The quantity and quality of information investors require today to make proper valuation of a company is constantly growing. With that, demands on the investor relations officers are increasing as well—professionals are required to understand every aspect of their company's business, understand its position in the industry, and be able to discuss this information with investors and analysts in compliance with variety of laws and regulations that govern the financial markets.

CHAPTER 5

Legal Environment

Investor relations is a highly regulated activity in most of the countries. In the United States, the primary agency responsible for oversight of the stock market is the United States Securities and Exchange Commission (SEC). On the agency's website, the SEC states its main mission is "to protect investors, maintain fair, orderly, and efficient markets, and facilitate capital formation."[1] To achieve these goals, the SEC oversees the federal securities laws, maintains the disclosure of financial information by publicly traded companies, and can bring enforcement actions against violators of the securities law. The SEC works in close cooperation with several other U.S. government agencies, such as the Federal Reserve Board of Governors and the Department of Treasury.

Prior to 1933, the United States did not have a comprehensive regulation of the securities markets on the federal level. Instead, individual states were left to enact their own laws to protect their citizens against investment fraud. These state laws, referred to as Blue Sky Laws, were enacted in response to a growing number of fraudulent speculative schemes targeted at general population. The schemes were not backed up by any assets or reasonable plans—all the fraudulent claims were "out of the blue sky." Thus, these con artists were referred to as "blue sky merchants," and the state laws protecting against these blue sky schemes were labeled Blue Sky Laws.

Nevertheless, in the early 1930s it became apparent that state laws alone cannot combat the securities fraud. The development of communication and transportation networks made interstate securities offering and trade easily accessible to both general public and con artists. State laws, however, were inadequate in dealing with interstate fraud. The Federal Government needed to step in and did so by creating a federal agency to provide an oversight over the securities markets—the SEC.

The SEC is headed by five commissioners. The commissioners are appointed by the President of the United States for a five-year term. The SEC must be a bipartisan body. In order to achieve this, no more than three commissioners can belong to the same political party. One of commissioners is designated by the U.S. President to be the Chair of the Commission. As of March 2009, the Chair of the Commission is Mary L. Schapiro—the first female to become the head of the agency. The four other representatives are: Kathleen L. Casey (R), Troy A. Paredes (R), Luis A. Aguilar (D), and Elisse B. Walter (D). Today the SEC employs almost 3,500 people. The Commission's organization chart consists of four divisions and 19 offices. The Division of Corporate Finance is directly charged with overseeing corporate disclosure practices and making sure that all investors, from Wall Street financial analysts to retirees in rural Iowa, have equal access to the corporate financial information. The Division reviews required disclosure documents filed by companies planning to sell their securities to general public, as well as periodic disclosures by publicly traded corporations. The Division encourages corporations to provide extensive and timely information, both positive and negative, about a company's business to ensure that investors can make an educated decision whether to buy, hold, or sell securities of the company.

The SEC also maintains EDGAR: Electronic Data Gathering, Analysis and Retrieval system. All publicly traded companies are required to submit their financial information to EDGAR, and that information becomes available to anyone who has a computer with Internet connection. EDGAR, however, is a noninteractive system—the information is presented simply as text. In early 2009, the SEC introduced new regulations that starting from a fiscal period ending on or after June 15, 2009, all large companies must use the new system—IDEA: Interactive Data Electronic Application. IDEA relies on the new interactive data format —eXtensible Business Reporting Language (XBRL). All other companies will start using IDEA by June 2011.

The key pieces of legislature that govern securities markets today are Securities Act of 1933, Securities Exchange Act of 1934, Regulation FD, and Sarbanes-Oxley Act of 2002.

Securities Act of 1933 requires any original interstate sale or offer of securities to be registered. The goal of the registration is twofold: first, it allows the government to make sure that there is no deceit or fraud behind such offer of securities. Second, it allows the authorities to ensure that the company fully discloses any relevant information pertaining to such offer and thus enables investors to evaluate this offer properly. The Act describes in detail the registration process and information that must be filed. In general, the company must file a document called prospectus that describes the specific types of securities offered, information about the company and its business, information about the management, and the financial statements certified by independent accountants.

The act also provides some exceptions for companies to avoid the process of registration. Two most common exceptions often used by foreign companies are Rule 144A and Regulation S. Rule 144A stipulates that foreign companies can be exempt from the registration process if they do not offer their securities to private individuals in the United States but only to large institutional investors. The SEC refers to such investors as QIBs—Qualified Institutional Buyers. QIBs have over $100 million in assets and typically employ financial analysts who can request the information from the issuer, analyze the offer of securities, and make qualified decisions on valuation of such securities themselves. As a result, the SEC believes that QIBs do not require the same protection as private investors or small institutional investors have under the Securities Act of 1933.

Regulation S also allows an issuer to be exempt from the registration if the securities do not have a connection to the United States—in other words, the company is located outside of the United States and issues securities outside of the United States. In addition, the company does not engage in direct selling efforts to U.S. investors. Many foreign companies also rely on Regulation S to avoid the registration requirement especially when issuing Depositary Receipts.

If the previously described Securities Act of 1933 regulates the initial offer of securities, the Securities Exchange Act of 1934 aims at regulating secondary trade of securities. The act provides regulation of brokerage firms, transfer agents, clearing companies, stock exchanges, and so on. The act establishes the guidelines for periodic reporting of major corporations with more than $10 million in assets and with more than 500 shareholders. In addition to corporate reporting requirements, the Securities Exchange Act of 1934 regulates proxy solicitation for shareholders' meetings, offers to trade blocks of shares in excess of 5% of all outstanding shares, and trading of securities by people with connections to the company (so-called insider trading).

Although the Securities Act of 1933 and Securities Exchange Act of 1934 were primarily enacted to protect the interests of shareholders, it turned out that they do not protect all shareholders equally well. If we look back at the efficient market hypothesis discussed earlier in this book, one of the key assumptions of this hypothesis is equal access to information by all participants. However, quite often, the company would report the important information first to key analysts following its stock during a conference call or private meetings with institutional investors. Then, the information would trickle down the chain to smaller institutional investors, brokers, and private shareholders. Thus, large institutions such as Merrill Lynch, Wachovia, and Lehman Brothers would get access to any material information before other investors and would have a chance to receive higher returns on their investments by outperforming the market. The situation was unfair to private shareholders but there was no way to make information available to everybody from New York to California instantaneously.

The end of 1990s, however, brought the widespread adoption of the Internet. People became capable of accessing information themselves including directly from the SEC filings or companies' websites. In addition, more and more people were engaging in self trading of securities using online brokerage firms. They needed to have access to information at the same time as large institutional investors did. The inequalities in the stock market became painfully obvious, and the government had to step in. As a result, the SEC adopted a new rule, Regulation FD (Fair Disclosure), in October 2000.

The key stipulation of Regulation FD was to eliminate the practice of "selective disclosure"—in other words, disclosure of information to some select parties (largely, institutional investors). Instead, Regulation FD requires the following:

> The regulation provides that when an issuer, or person acting on its behalf, discloses material nonpublic information to certain enumerated persons (in general, securities market professionals and holders of the issuer's securities who may well trade on the basis of the information), it must make public disclosure of that information.[2]

Such disclosure must also be done simultaneously to securities market professionals and everybody else, thus eliminating the opportunity for professional investors to "beat the market" by receiving information earlier. Regulation FD also provides provision for unintentional disclosure of information, in which case the company must follow up with the public disclosure in a very limited timeframe.

Although Regulation FD led to a significant improvement in the disclosure practices, it did not eliminate the problem completely. The competition among financial analysts pushes them to seek privileged information testing investor relations officers and executives almost daily through e-mails, phone calls, and one-on-one meetings. Regulators do not enforce the provision of Regulation FD very strictly either, creating a situation when it becomes an obligation of the investor relations officers to balance the demands of financial analysts and investors with the stipulations of the Regulation FD.

Finally, the most recent piece of legislature is the Sarbanes-Oxley Act. This new law, Public Company Accounting Reform and Investor Protection Act, was enacted July 30, 2002. It is often referred to by the name of its sponsors: Senator Paul Sarbanes (D-MD) and Representative Michael G. Oxley (R-OH), as Sarbanes-Oxley Act, or simply SOX. President George W. Bush, when signing the law, stated that Sarbanes-Oxley is "the most far-reaching reforms of American business practices since the time of Franklin D. Roosevelt." Others also call SOX "a most welcome gift to shareholders"[3]

SOX primarily focuses on further improving the quality and quantity of financial disclosure. To some extent, SOX was a governmental response to a wave of corporate scandals that shook corporate America at the beginning of the twenty first century. Many of these scandals were directly related to senior management's manipulation of information disclosed to investors and, as a result, the inability of investors, both private and corporate, to properly understand the company's business and its value. In the chain of corporate scandals even the companies once believed to be among the leaders in their respective fields, such as Adelphia, Global Crossings, WorldComm, Tyco International, Kmart, and Waste Management, experienced significant drops in their share prices and some even bankruptcies. Of course, the largest scandal of all was Enron: "The collapse of energy giant Enron is the largest bankruptcy and one of the most shocking failures in U.S. corporate history." Enron is referred to as "the Watergate of business."[4] The government had to restore the confidence of domestic and international investors in the very model of American capitalism.

SOX became the key step in restoring the investors' confidence. First, SOX creates Public Company Accounting Oversight Board (PCAOB), an independent board charged with improving the audit process. As described earlier, in accordance with Securities Acts of 1933 and Securities Exchange Act of 1934, public companies must have their financials verified by an independent accountant. PCAOB's goal is then to regulate the process of such audits and the companies that provide them. SOX creates specific requirements for auditing companies and explains what an auditor's independence from the company means.

SOX also expands the scope of disclosure by public companies. The enhanced disclosure includes off-balance-sheet transactions, liabilities, and obligations. The company must also report on the transactions carried out by company's executives.

SOX emphasizes the accuracy and completeness of the disclosure by public companies and introduces personal responsibility of the senior corporate managers for such disclosure. Specifically, Section 302 requires senior executives to certify the following:

- The signing officers have reviewed the report
- The report does not contain any material untrue statements or material omission or be considered misleading
- The financial statements and related information fairly present the financial condition and the results in all material respects
- The signing officers are responsible for internal controls and have evaluated these internal controls within the previous ninety days and have reported on their findings
- A list of all deficiencies in the internal controls and information on any fraud that involves employees who are involved with internal activities
- Any significant changes in internal controls or related factors that could have a negative impact on the internal controls[5]

The variety of other SOX provisions detail specific requirements for establishing internal structures to facilitate these new disclosure procedures, introduce corporate and criminal fraud accountability, and enhance white collar crime penalties.

Some of SOX's critics point out to the significant expense of compliance with the new requirements that SOX introduced. Creating the internal control structures and hiring an expensive audit company might become a cost-burden for smaller, publicly traded companies. However, others claim that this is money well spent and that it is worth paying for enhanced understanding of the company's business by shareholders and improved transparency of the market in general.

CHAPTER 6

Ethics and Professionalism

As explained above, the roles and functions of investor relations as a profession are closely tied to changes in economy and society in general. The very appearance of investor relation departments was caused by pressure from social movement activists and financial analysts: "Whereas social movement activists framed shareholder rights as a problem and compelled organizations to uphold them, professional analysts subtly coerced organizations to signal their commitment to investor rights by creating boundary-spanning structures."[1]

In other words, not only companies increased their shareholder's base, but social movement activists framed the relationship with shareholders as important and thus called for investor relations. A study of investor relations practices in Japan arrives at similar conclusions when Yoshikawa suggests that changes in the ownership structures and corporate finance practices require companies to engage in communication with their investors.[2] It is quite important because it means investor relations cannot be equated with just disclosure. The profession must move beyond mere publishing of financial information. In fact, investor relations ethical obligation becomes upholding the shareholder rights the activists demanded:

Investors truly indeed need an investor relations professional inside the corporate structure to protect their interests:

Ethical problem associated with shareholders arises from the nature of the agency relationship between shareholders and managers. The capitalist system is driven by an implicit assumption that people are driven by their legitimate self-interest. Agency theory, the theoretical foundation of much of academic accounting, assumes that managers are self-interested and are not burdened by ethical considerations; therefore, the central problem for shareholders is to put controls in place to ensure that managers do not expropriate excessively the shareholders' wealth for themselves.[3]

Investor relations officer becomes one of such controls. The investor relations job is to represent the interest of shareholders within the management team. When a company is considering a decision that can affect shareholders in a negative way, it is an ethical and professional responsibility of the investor relations officer to participate in a discussion by providing the perspective of shareholders. This can save a company from future shareholder lawsuits or aggressive shareholder activism at the next annual meeting. In a sense, investor relations officers serve as internal activists—if necessary fighting against top management decisions in the board room in order to protect the interests of shareholders. Mark Aaron, VP of Investor Relations at Tiffany & Co. states, "IR is not a role for someone who lacks courage to speak up."[4]

The loyalty of the investor relations officers lies not only with shareholders but with the company as well. In fact, investor relations officers are representatives of shareholders in the company's board room, but they are also representatives of their company among the shareholders. Once the company's decision was made with the best interests of all stakeholders taken into account, it becomes a job of the investor relations officer to explain this decision to the shareholders and financial analysts. In the complexity of corporate business models, the benefits or drawbacks of different decisions are not always obvious.

Indeed, not clearly understanding a company's business model is one of the main reasons why investors choose not to invest in a company's stock.[5] It is essential to present all the complexity of the company's business operations in a simplified and yet comprehensive picture. Executives tend to disclose too little information or disclose too much, overcrowding the data with nonrelevant noise. The professional responsibility of the investor relations officers is to identify and maintain the perfect informational balance that would be the most beneficial for investors and financial analysts.

Once the company made a decision, investor relations officers would need to deliver this decision to investors and explain all the details of such decision and how it will affect the company's business model in the short- and long-term future. The investor relations officers may be required to educate shareholders on the reasons behind such decisions and to defend the company's decisions against shareholders' criticism if such decision is in the best interests of the company.

In a sense, investor relations officers are taking on a role of "devil-advocates"—providing the opposite perspective both in the boardroom and among the shareholders. This is not an easy role, but it is the role that can help a company establish a competitive advantage through investor relations. After all, corporate lawyers, for example, are paid to disagree with the management if the management decision violates laws and regulations. The lawyer who would agree with the management all the time would be useless at best or criminal in the worst case scenario. The same is true for investor relations. By knowing the company's investors well, investor relations officers can foresee the reactions and objections of shareholders to the corporate plans and thus ensure that top management, when making such plans, takes the interests of shareholders in mind.

The key loyalty of the investor relations professionals, then, lies not with the management of the company and not even with the shareholders, but rather with the profession of investor relations itself and its role in the society. Medical doctors, for example, when treating a patient should not let their decisions be guided by insurance companies or hospital costs, despite the fact that hospitals and insurance companies are the ones paying their salary. Medical decisions should not follow the wishes of a patient, either—no matter how much the patient wants to smoke or drink alcohol, if it puts a patient's life at risk, it is a professional responsibility of doctors to inform the patient about it and demand the patient stops such behavior. The same is true for the investor relations professionals—it is important to stand up to the management and defend the interest of shareholders as much as it is important to stand up to the shareholders if their actions can damage company's ability to generate long-term value.

It is also an ethical obligation of the investor relations officers to lead both corporate executives and shareholders to take a note of the important issues left under radar. Today, for example investor relations officers put on the agenda issues of corporate social responsibility and environmental sustainability. Not all investors and not all executives perceive these issues as relevant. Yet such issues as gas emissions, climate change risks, and sustainable social practices may threaten the long-term success or even existence of corporations. Investor relations should raise these issues in the boardrooms and in meeting with shareholders, ensuring that all parties involved understand the importance of these issues and how corporations plans on dealing with them. There is hardly any doubt that eventually such disclosure will be mandated. Presently, however, it is the responsibility of the investor relations officers to ensure their companies are doing all they can to guarantee sustainable growth for centuries to come and educate investors and executives about these issues.

As a result, investor relations officers serve their companies, their companies' shareholders, and society at large. Thus, developing a sense of professionalism is essential for a successful investor relations officer. Investor relations officers should have an investor relations education, should be members of the professional organization, such as National Investor Relations Institute, and should stay up-to-date with the changing environment of the profession.

CHAPTER 7

Main Activities

On a day-by-day basis, investor relations officers produce annual reports, issue media releases, and conduct shareholder research. Laskin inquired what activity investor relations officers perform most often. He presented investor relations officers from Fortune 500 companies with a list of investor relations activities and asked them to rate how often they are involved in these tasks. The list included report preparations (annual reports, quarterly reports, and other reports), ownership research and analysis, controlled media communications (newsletters, mailing lists, web site postings, etc.), mass media communications (editorials, interviews, or advertising), group communications (roadshows or conference presentations), one-on-one communications and negotiations, responding to requests from shareholders and financial analysts, providing information to the executives and other departments of their organizations, compliance with regulations, and various management tasks.

Laskin's research concluded that the most common investor relations activity is responding to requests they receive from various constituencies. Indeed, hardly a day goes by without a financial analyst from a sell-side or buy-side contacting an investor relations officer. In fact, Laskin research concluded that institutional investors and financial analysts combined consume on average 70% of the investor relations officers' time.[1]

Financial analysts want to stay up-to-date on every development of the company: a launch of a new product, entering new markets, or hiring a new person to a top management team. Private shareholders also submit a fair share of requests for information. In fact, some organizations create a separate department to communicate with private shareholders in order to allow investor relations officers to have more time for financial analysts and professional investors.

Spending most of the time on responding to previously submitted requests raises a concern about the reactive nature of investor relations.

Indeed, if the focus of investor relations is on catching up with requests it does not leave much time for proactive and strategic planning for the benefit of the organization. In fact, controlled media communications, such as websites, mailings lists, newsletters, or other company's media that might allow investor relations officers to set an agenda and proactively deliver information to the interested parties, are rarely mentioned by the investor relations officers as the activity they are involved in.[2] Indeed, investor relations officers are often consumed by technical rather than strategic activities. Even today "an exclusive emphasis on intended technical activities deflects attention from the symbolic nature of investor relations departments and the institutional sources of organizational structure."[3] On the other hand, investor relations officers report that they are also often involved in roadshows, presentations, and conferences.[4] This indicates a proactive focus of the profession. Practiced proactively, investor relations can create a competitive advantage for a corporation.

Another interesting finding is involvement in one-on-one meetings. One-on-one meetings with investors or analysts have long been considered a cornerstone of investor relations. Yet it turns out involvement in one-on-one meetings depends on who manages the investor relations program. Investor relations officers managed by the corporate communication/public relations departments are not as often involved in one-on-meetings as officers managed by finance/treasury departments or as officers from a stand-alone investor relations departments. Investor relations officers from communication/public relations departments are also more often involved in the controlled media communications and performing managing tasks than officers from finance/treasury departments or stand-alone investor relations departments.[5]

Investor relations officers are also charged with keeping management up-to-date about the shareholders of the company. Investor relations officers constantly conduct ownership research and provide information to the top management or other departments of the organization. This confirms that the two-way communication is in the very nature of investor relations, when information is not traveling simply from organizations through the investor relations officer to target publics, but when investor relations professionals also deliver information from the investors, financial analysts, or brokers back to the management of their organizations. This emphasizes an important function for investor relations—counseling the management. Thus, two-way communications, an ideal for strategic communications, seems to be incorporated in the very nature of investor relations. It is important for the top-management to know who owns the company, who trades the stock, and what are their motivations; shareholder research is not uncommon in the investor relations. Investor relations practitioners are required not only to deliver the company's message to the shareholders but also to learn the shareholders position and present it to the company's top-management. National Investor Relations Institute (NIRI) recommends that "the company's investor relations officer . . . [should] report feedback from investors and analysts."[6]

What stands behind all these activities investor relations officers engage in? Needless to say, it is providing accurate and timely information to the financial community. But there is more to that. Private shareholders, institutional investors, and even financial analysts following the company are not as knowledgeable about the company's history, future aspirations, competitive position, and so on. It is not always sufficient to provide information to the investors. Often, investor relations officers are required to educate investors and analysts about the actions the company takes and what these actions mean for the future growth of the company. Explaining to investors complex research and development spending, new product offerings, or even new hires is an important aspect of the investor relations officer's job. Investor relations professionals cannot simply make information available to investors; they must make sure the information is understood correctly. Investor relations is not about disclosure of information; it is about understanding the company. Thus, investor relations officers from "disclosure" officers must often become "education" officers.

Proper understanding of a company's business, however, is not a goal in itself either. Rather, it is a stepping stone on the way to a bigger goal—building relationships with the financial community.

CHAPTER 8

Focus on Relationship Building

Among the problems investor relations executives consider important for the future of the investor relations profession, one of the most important is the short-term fixation of shareholders.[1] Short-termism of investors can harm companies. Wolff-Reid explains, "In recent years, Wall Street's obsession with beating quarterly numbers has been a destructive force, pushing companies to focus on short-term results down to penny."[2] Thus, it becomes an investor relations' responsibility to extend the horizon of the investors, or, as Bill Nielsen, a former Johnson & Johnson's vice president, phrases it, "Turning stock-holders into stock-owners." Communicating information beyond the U.S. generally accepted accounting principles (GAAP) requirements helps to achieve this goal by building a deeper understanding of the company's future and thus building a relationship between investors and a company. One of the anonymous investor relations practitioners in Laskin's study on the value of investor relations elaborates,

> Since we have invested the time and effort in building relationships . . . we are given the opportunity to explain our results and strategies more fully, and have a better chance to be given the benefit of the doubt in situations where investors and analysts are being asked to trust your word than if we didn't establish the relationship. [3]

Increasing the holding period and amount of ownership in the company can help stabilize the share price volatility and thus is a part of investor relations job. Such holding pattern is sometimes referred to as *relational investing.*[4] Investor relations academics and practitioners know of benefits of relational investing:

> The rewards of this relationship can be significant. Value gaps tend to diminish because investors believe management can accomplish what it says. Positive events and development earn higher stock gain rewards. A flat or down quarter isn't an automatic sell signal. Investors look for explanations and, when convinced that fundamentals are still strong and growing, are more likely to hold their shares or even increase their positions. Patience is more likely to be accorded.[5]

An academic study that analyzed relational investing noted that although the term becomes quite common, there is no precise definition for this phenomenon:

> The proponents of relational investing do not define who counts as relational investor, beyond the vague requirement that the investor hold a large block for a substantial time and actively monitor the firm's performance, nor do they specify how quickly the results of the investor's monitoring should show up in a firm's performance.[6]

The development of such relational approach parallels a similar approach in marketing, where the 1980s and 1990s brought a shift from transaction-oriented marketing to relationship-oriented marketing.[7]

Others use a similar term, *relationship investing*, and define it the following way: "Simply put, whenever there's an established, committed link between a company and one or more shareholders, that's relationship investing."[8] Relationship investing, thus, becomes synonymous to relational investing. They both mean long-term investing, investing in a large share of a company's stock, and finally active monitoring of the corporate actions.

As mentioned earlier, this can create several benefits for the company in the long run: "First, it helps solve a problem executives have complained about for years: short-term investing. By creating a class of enlightened investors who give companies patient capital, relationship investing should free management to focus on the long term."[9] This long-term focus should enable the company to invest in such activities as, for example, research and development, thus improving the firm's competitiveness in the long run.

Furthermore, "the very existence of a new breed of active capitalists fixes another failing of U.S. corporations: the imperial CEO, unchecked by a pliant board of directors. . . . Investors who actively monitor their holdings would introduce a badly needed measure of management accountability."[10] An academic study analyzed several cases of investors getting closely involved with the companies (e.g., Avon, Kodak, Sears, Lockheed) and all these cases improved their corporate performance after active involvement of shareholders in company's activities.[11] Across the literature, there is "a variety of evidence, some systematic and some anecdotal" that can support the claim that long-term investing can lead to improvements in corporate performance.[12]

So, relational investors instead of "trading stock like pork bellies" exhibit a real long-term interest in the company, its management, the way it is run, and the way the company communicates with them. Relational investors are the ones who want to influence the company's management and provide advice on how the company should be run. They are also often the ones who have the power to assert such an influence. Relational investing requires the presence of a strong, competent, and influential shareholder.[13] As a result, relational investing is an underlying reason behind shareholder's activism, a sign of shareholders' involvement in the company's future. The presence of a strong shareholder that can and want to influence the company's decision-making process might cause panic for some managers.[14] On the other hand, companies that pay attention to the expertise and knowledge of such shareholders are often rewarded with long-term, sustainable financial success.[15] In simple terms, relational investors provide patient capital in exchange for increased accountability.

The terms *relational investing* and *relationship investing*, however, both look at the issue from the standpoint of the investment community. Analyzing the same issue from the standpoint of a corporation and its investor relations practitioners, this issue can be labeled *investor relationship*. The term would encompass the efforts of the investor relations professionals to recruit or develop long-term relational investors for their companies by building relationships between shareholders and the company. Thus, the term *investor relationship* builds on the traditional corporate function of *investor relations* but places an emphasis on the importance of developing relationships with shareholders, helping them to become *relational investors* or engaging them in *relationship investing.*

The benefits of investor relationship are not limited to just corporations and investment community. In fact, relational investing has a potential of solving the common problem of investors' *rational apathy*— a situation in which investors prefer to withdraw from the company (selling the stock) if faced with a problem, bad corporate practices, or unethical behavior.[16] The group of experts on corporate law charged by the European Commission with the task of researching corporate practices in Europe concludes,

> From the viewpoint of a single shareholder, it may frequently seem appropriate to sell his shares if he is dissatisfied with—or lacks confidence in—incumbent management, rather than try to change things within the company. However, this "rational apathy" may prove very disadvantageous if adopted as a general attitude among shareholders.[17]

Relational investors, however, do not sell the stock in a similar situation. Rather, they try to communicate their dissatisfaction to management and persuade the company to change its policies. In other words, instead of fleeing from the problem, relational investors work on solving it. These investors provide their skills, knowledge, and expertise to the company and thus can potentially lead to improvements on the company's side. Such investors strive to get above-average returns from their investment in *the company*, not from their investment in *the market.*

Investor relationship, however, heavily relies on the extensive disclosure that goes beyond minimum U.S. GAAP requirements. Strategic investors need to understand the company as well as managers do and as a result want additional information. Thus, extended disclosure of both financial and nonfinancial information is an essential part of investor relationship.

CHAPTER 9

Focus on Extended Disclosure

Investor relations today experience many changes caused by the changes in the economy, regulations, and the role of corporation in society. But one of the main factors fueling these changes is a shift to intangibles. Steve Wallman, a former SEC Commissioner, claims, "When historians look back at the turn of the century, they will note one of the most profound economic shifts of the era: The rise of Intangible Economy."[1]

The role of intangible assets and nonfinancial indicators for present-day corporations is constantly growing:

> Wealth and growth in modern economies are driven primarily by intangible assets, defined as: claims to future benefits that do not have a physical or financial form. Patents, bioengineering drugs, brands, strategic alliances, customer lists, a proprietary cost-reducing Internet-based supply chain—these are all examples of intangibles assets. The more traditional physical and financial assets are rapidly becoming commodities, since they are equally accessible to competitors, and consequently yield at best a competitive return on investment. Dominant market positions, abnormal profits, and even temporary monopolistic advantage are today most effectively achieved by the sound deployment of intangible assets.[2]

In other words, not only is the role of intangibles increasing, but the role of tangible assets is simultaneously diminishing as they become less and less capable of creating a competitive advantage and, thus, providing above-average returns.

This role of intangibles makes them an important contributor to understanding a value of a company. In fact, some scholars claim that intangible assets "account for well over half the market capitalization of public companies."[3] In fact, the market value of many corporations today significantly exceeds their "hard" assets even taking into account the difference between current market price of assets and the historical cost-based accounting. In total, the market value of all U.S. publicly traded companies is about "five times larger than their balance sheet value, which reflects primarily the net worth of physical and financial assets."[4] For Internet-related companies, the market price can exceed their "hard" assets value 100 times or more.

The importance of intangible assets and nonfinancial indicators of corporate performance is not escaping managers who readily recognize that intangibles are important to their company's success. Financial analysts and professional investors also realize the importance of nonfinancial information for proper evaluation of a company. Ernst & Young conducted a series of surveys and experiments with financial analysts to discover that nonfinancial information has a significant influence in stock analysis and its importance is high.[5] In fact, financial analysis of the company's value is heavily dependent on the proper understanding of the contribution of intangibles:

> The greatest part of the analysis is based upon intangibles and unmeasurable factors, such as management and the company's ability to plan and meet its objectives. The more precisely and clearly the elements that define these intangibles are projected, the more readily the company's ability to appreciate the invested dollar will be understood. The more readily this ability is understood, the more likely the acceptance—and the investment—by a financial community that discounts for the unknown—the risk.[6]

This means that intangibles should take the central role in "valuation calculus preformed by investors."[7]

No doubt that traditional financial disclosure is still important. However, investors want to also understand what stands behind the numbers. Intangibles are the cause of the revenue stream and thus create a better and deeper understanding of the company's business model. Intangibles are the foundation of the company's business model, underlying reason for its success or failure. Financial statements, then, become the applications—how well the business idea is being managed and implemented.

Investors also realize this importance of intangibles and nonfinancial factors: "Investors give nonfinancial measures, on average, one-third of the weight when making a decision to buy or sell any given stock."[8] Thus, to better educate investors and shareholders about the company and to create a true understanding of the company, investor relations officers must be proficient at communicating intangibles to the financial publics.

Two accounting professors, Ittner and Larcker, in an article in *Financial Times* argue that intangibles and nonfinancial measures can be better predictors of financial performance of companies than financial indicators if taken in the long term:

> Even when the ultimate goal is maximizing financial performance, current financial measures may not capture long-term benefits from decisions made now. Consider, for example, investments in research and development or customer satisfaction programs. Under U.S. accounting rules, research and development expenditures and marketing costs must be charged for in the period they are incurred, so reducing profits. But successful research improves future profits if it can be brought to market. Similarly, investments in customer satisfaction can improve subsequent economic performance by increasing revenues and loyalty of existing customers, attracting new customers and reducing transaction costs. Nonfinancial data can provide the missing link between these beneficial activities and financial results by providing forward-looking information on accounting or stock performance.[9]

In other words, investors and analysts, trying to predict the future financial performance of companies, have a better chance of getting it right if they take into account various nonfinancial indicators.

Yet surprisingly, despite the recognized importance, neither managers nor investors can manage, communicate, or evaluate intangibles as well as they can manage, communicate, and evaluate tangible assets. Several research projects conducted by Lev and his colleagues indicated that "investors systematically misprice the shares of intangibles-intensive enterprises."[10] The questions, however, arises as to why this mispricing occurs? Who or what is responsible for that "underpricing securities and misallocating corporate resources mean that both companies and investors are leaving substantial value on the table. Why would rational people give up large potential gains from optimal investments in intangibles?"[11]

The answer might lie in inability of investors, essentially outsiders of the company, to fully grasp the value of complex intangible profit-making capabilities. Or in time constraints of financial analysts who have to cover many corporations and digest large amounts of information to present their recommendations to the investors and thus often resort to simplified financial models that do not take into account much of intangibles value. Often the answer lies also in the lack of disclosure about intangibles assets and their value-creating contribution to the organizational business processes in the information that IROs provide to the financial markets. Such shortage of information can no doubt harm investors' understanding and subsequent evaluation of intangibles: "Look carefully beneath the shiny veneer of intangibles and you will find a knotty and unattractive reality, one in which information deficiencies both at companies and in the capital markets feed negatively on one another."[12]

The lack of disclosure to investors about the company's intangible assets is an important contributor to the problem: "It is widely agreed that corporate financial reports provide deficient information about intangible assets."[13] However, it is unlikely to be the only reason. Another issue is the complexity and difficulty of evaluating these assets. One might argue that the burst of the dot-com bubble was partially caused by the inability of financial analysts and investor to correctly evaluate business models built on intangible assets:

> Although managers and financial analysts intuitively perceive the importance of intangibles to business success, they currently lack knowledge about the systematic findings of research into the economic attributes of intangibles, particularly regarding measurement and evaluation. As a result, the management of intangibles and the investment valuation of intangible-intensive companies tend to be haphazard. For example, there are no widely accepted tools available with which a manager might assess the return on

investments in intangibles (R&D, brands, employee training). Similarly, investor valuations of intangible-intensive firms are inadequate, leading to a systematic mispricing of securities and excessive stock price volatility.[14]

In addition to the lack of informative disclosures and lack of measurement matrix, intangibles are suffering from the inability to be evaluated by comparison. In fact, there are hardly ever comparables for intangible assets. Indeed, with tangible assets, investors can often rely on the market prices of such assets because there is a market for land, office space, cars, oil, tools, and other means of production. This helps to evaluate and compare the companies. When intangibles are involved, however, it is rare to find comparable intangibles traded on an open market. Even more, often such intangibles are unique to a specific firm and cannot be transferred to another corporation—like a unique organizational structure or historical ties with a supplier.

Lack of timely, extensive, and accurate disclosure of nonfinancial indicators, inability to measure their value, and nonexistence of market prices and comparables can lead to systematic undervaluation of intangibles causing the companies to suffer by harming their cost of capital and limiting their growth potential. An academic research project analyzed a sample of R & D–intensive companies from 1983 to 2000 and discovered that this underpricing of firms with heavy contribution of intangible assets to the corporate bottom line is, in fact, not random.[15] Research and development, one of the intangible activities, can potentially generate a substantial value for a company and, subsequently, its investors. But can investors recognize that?

If investors are capable of evaluating R & D activities fairly, then return on R & D–intensive stocks should not differ significantly from returns on the market; in other words, the stock market should fully reflect the future potential of such stocks. Yet study after study discovers that research and development stocks are constantly underpriced "as evidenced by the protracted large and positive returns over several years following portfolio formation."[16]

Another reason for the lack of understanding and misevaluation of intangibles is the serious deficiencies and inadequacies in U.S. GAAP's accounting standard when it comes to intangibles. Modern accounting standards do not include nonfinancial indicators of corporate performance and do not require the companies to disclose much information on intangibles. In this situation, a complete GAAP revision might be required:

> But generally accepted accounting principles perpetuate the information deficiency. GAAP treats practically all internally generated intangibles not as investments but as costs that must be immediately expensed, thereby seriously distorting enterprise profitability and asset value. Furthermore, GAAP does not require firms to disclose any meaningful information about intangibles investments, except for aggregate R&D expenditures, lumping the rest of them in with general expenses. This keeps investors in the dark about, for example, how companies allocate R&D budgets to basic research, product development, and process improvements— not to mention the amounts being invested in a host of other intangibles, including software development and acquisitions, brand enhancement, and employee training. The financial reports likewise provide no information on revenue generated by these investments, such as patent-licensing fees or the share of revenues coming specifically from new products. No wonder, then, that investors, trapped in their forced ignorance about intangibles, apply an excessive uncertainty discount to the shares of intangibles-intensive enterprises. In capital markets, no news is bad news.[17]

In other words, investors have to estimate the value of intangibles without having any information about them—an impossible task. The companies are not required to disclose nonfinancial indicators to help investors in their efforts to understand corporate business models, earnings potential, or long-term vision.

Although not included in GAAP, intangibles can be a significant contributor to the value and thus omitting such contribution can render the whole financial reporting irrelevant. This creates an accounting paradox: "Internally developed intangible assets . . . are generally not permitted by generally accepted accounting standards (GAAP) to be recognized in the financial statements, but instead are immediately expensed. These assets, such as patents, technology and brand names, are often of significant value to a company." As a result, the whole idea of usefulness and relevance of accounting reports to investors could be questioned.[18]

Various non-GAAP and internal performance measures also often suffer from similar fallacies—almost exclusive focus on the financial results. Such overreliance on financial measures versus drivers of value contributes to a short-term and narrow-focused investment perception. Indeed, Enron showed investors that it is possible to manipulate the numbers in the short term when managers are pressured to meet the monthly, quarterly, or annual targets. Focusing on the numbers limits the scope of the company activities and does not explain how these numbers were created: "Numbers are not the most complete or appropriate measure to demonstrate organizational performance. . . . Financial measures also can be manipulated to meet the outcomes desired by the party reporting them."[19]

Perhaps overreliance on the financial indicators is the remnant of not-so-distant past, the industrial era of development:

> Executives also understand that traditional financial accounting measures like return on investment and earnings per share can give misleading signals for continuous improvement and innovation—activities today's competitive environment demands. The traditional financial performance measures worked well for the industrial era, but they are out of step with the skills and competencies companies are trying to master today.[20]

As a result, if the investor relations function aims at building an improved understanding of the company and its business model, this becomes a job of the investor relations officers to present, explain, and educate investors on the value of intangibles the company has and is developing, as well as these intangibles' contribution to the overall business model and value of the corporation:

> Many non-financial factors have demonstrated that they contribute to and have a lasting impact on a company's market value. Since these non-financial measures are more forward-looking and are linked to operational activities, they help to focus a manager's

efforts and better evaluate employee performance. . . . Managers can no longer afford to hang on to preconceived notions of financial measures as the holy grail of organizational accountability. Integrating non-financial measures regarding the strategic performance of the organization will help to communicate objectives, assist in the effective implementation of strategic plans and provide incentive for management to address long-term strategy.[21]

This means that corporate executives must pay more attention to intangibles and nonfinancial measures to evaluate performance. The same claim can be extended to investors—who also must rely on intangibles to evaluate the performance of corporations. Investors, however, do not have such an easy access to the data about intangibles and non-financial measures—they are in a certain information vacuum because of inadequate disclosure as it relates to intangibles. Thus, it becomes an important part of the investor relations officer's job to compensate this lack of information about intangible drives of corporate performance by enhancing the scope of information provided to investors and analysts. The nonfinancial indicators that carry information on the company's corporate strategy, management, organizational capital, employees, research and development, market position, quality of products and services, and corporate social responsibility can satisfy this informational void and help investors and analysts value the company fairly.

This importance of intangibles and, subsequently, the need for disclosing nonfinancial indicators is only going to increase with time as commodization of physical assets will diminish their contribution to the corporations' value-generation potential and bring the competition into the intangibles sphere. Today, intangibles are not limited to so-called new technology companies but rather become a foundation for creating value in every industry from retail to mining.

Therefore, intangibles become an important part of investor communications for publicly traded companies in every industry. Intangibles are creating competitive advantages for companies and as a result intangibles are the foundation of companies' business models. Intangibles underlie the financial results and thus understanding a company requires understanding its intangibles. Intangibles allow investor relations officers to better explain the financial results and company's prospects for future growth. Intangibles also focus attention on long-term performance and are better aligned with long-term organizational strategies and objectives instead of short-term financial results. Finally, intangibles help cultivate long-term relationship with the investors and shareholders. Consequently, it becomes important for investor relations to have a clear understanding what the terms *intangibles* and *nonfinancials* mean in regards to investor relations and communicating with the financial public.

CHAPTER 10

Focus on Nonfinancial Information

Many scholars and professionals argue for the increased role of intangibles and nonfinancial indicators in evaluating the corporate performance. At the same time, scholars and professionals also observe a problem with these measures: lack of consistency. Variety of aspects that can be measured, different scales of measurement, different timeframes, and other issues cause confusion instead of improved understanding of the company's business.[1] Thus, it becomes essential to analyze and classify what exactly is meant by intangibles.

Intangibles and nonfinancial indicators are often used interchangeably. In fact, indicators that measure intangibles are often called nonfinancial indicators. It is important to note, however, that quite often it is a convention rather than fact. Indeed, many intangibles can be expressed in financial terms. Brand, for instance, is an intangible factor, yet Interbrand successfully measures the value of such intangible factor in financial terms and over time. For example, the value of Coca-Cola brand, the most expensive brand according to the 2007 study, stands on $65,324 million, followed by Microsoft ($58,709 million), and IBM ($57,091 million).[2] Research and development, another intangible factor, is also measured in financial terms by various organizations with variable success.[3] Intangibles in general can be expressed in the financial terms. For example, a research project carried out by Nakamura estimates all capital stock of intangibles in the United States to exceed $5 trillion dollars, while annual investment in intangible to exceed $1 trillion.[4]

One of the most advanced programs of research on the subject of intangible assets was launched by Baruch Lev, who today is sometimes referred to as "the guru of intangibles."[5] Lev conducted numerous research projects to better understand the phenomenon of intangibles:

from general studies on defining intangibles,[6] measuring intangibles,[7] and analyzing value-generation capabilities of intangibles,[8] to specific aspects of intangibles such as research and development,[9] role of innovations in business,[10] and the role of intangibles in the collapse of Enron.[11]

Baruch Lev provides the following definition for intangible assets: "An intangible asset is a claim to future benefits that does not have a physical or financial (a stock or a bond) embodiment. A patent, a brand, and a unique organizational structure (for example, an Internet-based supply chain) that generates cost savings are intangible assets."[12] He often uses the terms *intangible assets*, *knowledge assets*, and *intellectual capital* interchangeably. Allan Greenspan pioneered another term, *conceptual assets*, which also can be used synonymously with intangibles assets.[13]

Lev identified four categories of intangibles assets:

- Products/services
- Customer relations
- Human resources
- Organizational capital[14]

The organizational capital category deals with all the business processes and corporate designs that help companies achieve above-average returns by increasing revenues or decreasing costs. Among examples of this category of intangibles are Wal-Mart's supply chain management, Dell's inventory and built-to-order computers, and Citibank's Internet banking. "Unique information processes, such as those of the Italian apparel manufacturer Benetton, relaying real-time information about product colors from stores to production facilities, provide another example of the intangible—organizational capital."[15] The commodization of physical assets makes access to them available for everybody and thus the only way for corporation to outperform the competition is to build unique organizational structure links between these assets, in other words to add the intangible component—the organizational capital.

Human resources category includes compensation systems and other employee incentives, training programs, recruitment and retention efforts, and so on. This type of intangibles is also capable of generating above-average returns. For example, a research project documents that when a firm transitioned from an hourly rate to compensation based on the number of units completed, employee productivity increased 41%. As a result, without any changes in the number of employees or facilities of any other tangible assets, the company increased its productivity through intangible asset, human resources.[16]

Customer relations category is closely related with such concepts as brand, product image, advertising, and public relations. "When a loyalty of customers to a product (e.g., Bayer aspirin) or a company enables a business enterprise to charge higher prices than its competitors charge or to secure a large market share (e.g., the investment bank Goldman Sachs) customer-related intangibles are present."[17]

Finally, product/services category of intangibles directly relates to company's outputs. Examples of intangible products include for example software products, financial services, leisure and entertainment, health services and similar. An important caveat is that the line between tangible and intangible products is often blurry. Software, for example, can be physically located on a CD, and thus have a tangible component. However, in this case, it is clear that the value for the customer lies in the intangible product, not in the tangible disk itself. In other instances it may not be clear cut. For example, a computer, a refrigerator, or an automobile are combinations of tangible and intangible products that cannot be separated from each other. "Intangibles are frequently embedded in physical assets (for example, the technology and knowledge contained in an airplane) and in labor (the tacit knowledge of employees), leading to considerable interaction between tangible and intangible assets in creation of value."[18]

The four categories of intangibles developed by Lev try to encompass all the variety of intangible assets to create a model for analyzing and evaluating them. This model, however, is not the only one developed for understanding intangibles. Another approach that received much attention in the professional community was developed and popularized by Robert Kaplan and David Norton.

Kaplan and Norton, similar to Lev, observed that financial measures alone are insufficient to understand and to manage the corporation. Their research resulted in creating the concept of the *Balanced Scorecard*, a measurement approach that takes into account both financial measures and nonfinancial measures. Their idea of the balanced scorecard was accepted exceptionally well. In fact, some claim that the balanced scorecard was one of the most influential ideas of the 21st century[19] and the major innovation in the performance measurement.[20] The American Accounting Association gave it an award for the best theoretical contribution to the profession.[21]

Kaplan and Norton, meanwhile, continued developing their idea. Developed initially as a measurement tool,[22] balanced scorecard evolved into the management tool that can allow managers to translate their strategies into actions of their employees.[23] Later, balanced scorecard became management and control system—an approach of mapping the assets and evaluating the performance based on financial and nonfinancial indicators to align the corporate actions with corporate strategy.[24] The industry widely accepted the idea—half of the *Global 1000* companies were using a balanced scorecard in one way or another by the year 2000.[25] Finally, "a recent Bain & Company survey of more than 708 companies on five continents found that the BSC [balance scorecard] was used by 62% of responding organizations, a higher adoption rate than some other well-known management tools like Total Quality Management, Supply Chain Integration or Activity Based Management."[26]

The roots of the balanced scorecard, however, can be traced back to times long before 1992, using a similar management tool pioneered in France in 1930s under the name *tableau de board*, or *dashboard*.[27] This dashboard allowed managers to monitor various aspects of performance of different units in addition to financial aspects. The *dashboard* concept received much attention in both the industry and academic research in France and is in fact used even today by French corporations. Perhaps the language barrier was the main reason in preventing the dashboard concept from entering the U.S. professional and academic literature.[28] In the United States, however, there were precursors to the balanced scorecard as well. The system similar to balanced scorecard was developed by General Electric back in 1950s.[29]

The balanced scorecard today is an opportunity to look beyond just financial results. In fact, it can show how organizational mission and strategy are being carried out by organizational actions. Indeed, it is impossible to measure the success of a business enterprise based on financial results alone as these can be a result of outside events or nonsustainable business practices, for example,

Think of the balanced scorecard as the dials and indicators in an airplane cockpit. For the complex task of navigating and flying a plane, pilots need detailed information about many aspects of the flight. They need information on fuel, airspeed, altitude, bearing, destination, and other indicators that summarize the current and predicted environment. Reliance on one instrument can be fatal. Similarly, the complexity of managing an organization today requires that managers be able to view performance in several areas at once.[30]

Thus, the balanced scorecard suggested expanding the scope of managerial attention from financial indicators to a variety of other performance measures. Kaplan and Norton identify four main categories of indicators in the balanced scorecard:

- Financial perspective
- Internal business perspective
- Customer perspective
- Innovation and learning perspective[31]

Financial perspective is the traditional measures of corporate performance: profitability, growth, shareholder value, and similar measures. Some of the common indicators are revenues, cash flow, sales growth, return on equity, and so on. Internal business perspective describes processes, decisions, and actions occurring throughout organizations. Some of the indicators for the internal business perspective include cycle time, unit costs, and efficiency. Customer perspective translates the corporate performance into customer-oriented measures, such as time-to-market of new products, defect level, on-time delivery, customer service, and so on. Some of the measures of customer perspective for the airline industry might be on-time arrivals and lost baggage, for example. The final perspective is innovation and learning perspective:

Intense global competition requires that companies make continual improvements to their existing products and processes and have the ability to introduce entirely new products with expanded capabilities. A company's ability to innovate, improve, and learn ties directly to the company's value.[32]

Example of the measures of product and process innovations can be time-to-develop, sales from new products, cycle time, and time-to-maturity.

In general, the balance scorecard should provide a balanced view of the business enterprise and allow managers and investors to correctly evaluate its success or failure and understand the reasons for such success or failure. As a result of bringing together these indicators, "the name [balance scorecard] reflected the balance between short- and long-term objectives, between financial and nonfinancial measures, between lagging and leading indicators, and between external and internal performance perspectives."[33]

It is important to note that there are significant parallels between Lev's research on intangibles and Kaplan and Norton's research on the nonfinancial indicators of the balanced scorecard. Kaplan and Norton's innovation and learning perspective is very similar to Lev's innovation-related intangibles. Lev's customer relations intangibles are similar to customer perspective of Kaplan and Norton. Kaplan and Norton's internal business perspective combines two types of intangibles from Lev's classification: organizational capital and human resources. In fact, the American Accounting Association that awards the Wildman Medal for the best fundamental research contribution to the accounting profession recognized both Lev and Kaplan with this medal in 2000 and 2001, respectively.

One of the many important contributions of Kaplan and Norton's work, however, is the recognition of the fact that both financial and nonfinancial indicators are closely related and that reliance on either one of them is erroneous. Instead of choosing between financial and operational measures, both perspectives are employed in evaluation of corporate performance. Tangible and intangible assets, financial and nonfinancial indicators are equally important for understanding the corporate performance and the corporate value.

Lev's analysis and Kaplan and Norton's body of research are not the only examples of classifications of intangibles. Auditing companies invested efforts into analyzing and categorizing intangible measures of corporate performance as well. One of the most sophisticated examples of such studies is Ernst & Young's *Measures That Matter* project.

Introducing the project, Ernst & Young, one of the world leading audit-ing companies, dedicates significant resources to a study of nonfinancial measures:

> Savvy corporate leaders seeking to meet the key management challenges of the future realize there is a dangerous disconnect between the bottom line and long-term goals. Sharing knowledge, wooing customers, and honing the products that will reinvent their industries represent investments for the long-term—usually at odds with short-term reporting practices. At the heart of this new thinking is a growing body of evidence revealing that reliance on financial measures alone will critically undermine the strategies leading-edge companies *must* [emphasis in the original] pursue to survive and thrive long term.[34]

Ernst & Young's study often refers to Baruch Lev's ideas, sometimes quoting his words; yet, they refer to their approach as balanced scorecard, similar to the Kaplan and Norton's terminology. Ernst & Young however extends the number of categories from four to eight:

- Quality of management
- Effectiveness of executive compensation policies
- Strength of corporate culture
- Level of customer satisfaction
- Strength of market position
- Quality of products and services
- Effectiveness of new product development
- Quality of investor communications

These eight groups do not really add many new dimensions to Lev's or Kaplan and Norton's classifications, but rather provide more details and specificity. Indeed, the first three categories, quality of management, executive compensation, and corporate culture, could all be summarized in Kaplan and Norton's internal business perspective or Lev's human resources type of intangibles. Kaplan and Norton's customer perspec-tive probably would include Ernst & Young's customer satisfaction, market position, and partially quality of products and services. All these categories are also similar to Lev's customer relations.

Ernst & Young, however, added a clearly new category, quality of investor communications. This category was not covered by Lev or by Kaplan and Norton as the only external communication streams they looked at were targeted at customers, not at shareholders or any other publics for that matter. Indeed, the relations with shareholders, government regulatory organizations, activist groups, and local community organizations can also have a strong and lasting impact on the corporate future and as a result should be accounted for.

Another advancement of the Ernst & Young research lies in the fact that they tested these nonfinancial measures with investors and financial analysts. The study analyzed over 300 sell-side investment reports to see how nonfinancial data were used, if used at all. "The findings are compelling. We learned that analysts do, in fact, rely strongly on a broad range of non-financial indicators."[35] The analysts relied mostly on the indicators related to customers and products, followed by indicators of quality of employees and other internal processes as well as factors of innovations. Ernst & Young also studied the usage of nonfinancial indicators by the buy-side through a survey of 275 portfolio managers. Once again, the results indicated the importance of intangibles for investors: "As with the sell-side study, we found that institutional investors not only pay attention to nonfinancial factors, but that they also apply the knowledge when making investment decisions." The report continues, "Well over 60% of survey respondents said that nonfinancial data drove between 20% and 50% of their investment decision."[36]

Finally, Ernst & Young went another step further and ranked different nonfinancial indicators between each other to find out which ones are the most important for investors and which ones are less important. As mentioned above, the Ernst & Young study had eight categories composed of 39 nonfinancial indicators overall, three to seven indicators per category. The most important for investors were strategy execution, management credibility, quality of strategy, innovativeness, and ability to attract talented people. All of these are long-term focused indicators, dealing with ability the company to meet its long-term goals as specified in the corporate strategy. The least important were compensation ratios, use of employee teams, and process quality awards—in other words, the indicators that are less strategic and more current or even focused in the past. The authors of the study also conducted an experiment, asking investors to analyze the companies based on several scenarios: In all scenarios nonfinancial information was the same but the financial results changes. The findings also showed that the more nonfinancial measures analysts use, the more accurate are their earnings forecasts.

So, the Ernst & Young's research had an important contribution to the study of intangibles. It showed that investors care about the nonfinancial information, they actively use that information in their analysis of companies, and that information helps them make the correct predictions. The most important of these nonfinancial are the ones related to top-management and long-term strategy of the corporation as it has the potential to affect the value of the company the most. The study's conclusions are profound: "Sell-side and buy-side investors alike make their own inferences about nonfinancial performance and then act upon these inferences, whether companies strategically manage and disclose nonfinancial factors or not." Thus, investor relations departments should manage this information as much as they manage financial disclosure in order "to gain or sustain a competitive edge."[37]

The research efforts conducted by academics and practitioners once again emphasize the important role of intangible assets and nonfinancial indicators. Yet these studies also highlight the complexity of intangibles and the difficulty of communicating them and properly evaluating them. It becomes an investor relations officer's responsibility to ensure shareholders and financial analysts are well aware of company's intangibles and their value-creating potential. This role of investor relations will only increase in the future as the importance of intangibles is increasing in the corporate value chains.

CHAPTER 11

Future of Investor Relations

There is no doubt investor relations as a profession will endure more changes in the future. The financial crisis that continues in the United States and around the world draws the attention of activists and legislators to the way financial markets operate. Some of the key changes that will have a significant impact on the profession in the nearest future are the advent of eXtensible Business Reporting Language (XBRL), the evolution of investor relations on the Internet, and the continued globalization of investment markets.

Imagine a press release where each word has an invisible tag. When a person receives this press release, every word is automatically placed in a proper cell—a row for nouns, a row for pronouns, a row for verbs, and so on. Now imagine instead of a press release it is a quarterly financial report. And instead of every word, every number has an invisible tag. When a financial analyst receives this information, numbers are automatically placed into proper cells in the financial analyst's Excel file, database, or a financial model. This is XBRL in the simplest terms—eXtensible Business Reporting Language. The financial reporting becomes automated and processed by a computer—the data can be streamed from the CFO's database straight to investors' or financial analysts' databases.

XBRL is the foundation for IDEA—Interactive Data Application Registrations. IDEA is the new database maintained by the Securities and Exchange Commission (SEC) with the purpose of providing information submitted by publicly traded companies, to investors, financial analysts, and any other interested parties. IDEA will be a replacement for EDGAR (Electronic Data Gathering, Analysis and Retrieval system), discussed in chapter 2. Since all filings in EDGAR were essentially text based and were primarily accessed as text documents, it was quite a painful process for investors and analysts to locate the information they were looking for. In fact, investors would often complain of information overload when a sentence of really useful information would be buried in pages of text that did not have any significance, such as legal caveats or repeats of previously disclosed information. Securities and Exchange Commissioner (SEC) Troy Paredes exclaimed in his speech, "Ironically, if investors are overloaded, more disclosure actually can result in less transparency and worse decisions!"[1]

IDEA will simplify this process. XBRL-based documents have the potential to enable advanced search functions as well as automated analysis and data manipulation. Even more, it will allow comparing data across companies and even industries based on the tags submitted within the XBRL documents.

Adoption of XBRL-based reporting causes some concerns as well. For example, no two companies are quite the same. On one hand, having standardized tags not only makes comparing across companies easier but it also may make it more difficult to describe the specific situation the company is in at the moment. On the other hand, expanding the amount and types of tags available for reporting helps each company in describing their specific situation but makes cross-company comparisons more difficult as they may be using different types of tags. Adding textual tags or tags like "other" can make standardization and comparisons between different companies or even between different years completely impossible.

Another issue is reporting of nonfinancial information in XBRL-based documents. Research and development expenses may put a company on a verge of technological breakthrough, but there is no tag in XBRL for a technological breakthrough. Standardization is difficult, if not impossible, in the world of nonfinancials and intangibles, yet as discussed in previous chapters, intangibles are playing more and more important role in the corporate value structure. How ready will XBRL be to deal with this information? How much of this value may be lost in the XBRL-based financial reporting and will be left for conference calls and meetings with the investors and analysts? Today, XBRL providers trying to move beyond the basic financials in XBRL tags meet substantial challenges, even when working on such tags as corporate action tags.

Despite these concerns, XBRL is here to stay and will no doubt change the way investor relations professionals go about their daily routine. XBRL can prove its worth by just increasing the accuracy of corporate disclosures and eliminating intermediary distortion. But investor relations will have to take the lead and help finance and treasury departments at their respective organizations to translate the company's financial picture into XBRL language in accordance with the latest government requirements. Investor relations professionals will also have to facilitate the interactions with investors and be prepared for any investors' concerns once XBRL reporting takes place.

Investors' meetings themselves may also look differently in the near future. Conference calls already cut down the travel budgets, but the next wave of shareholder interaction tools may push the envelope even further. The SEC encourages the use of electronic communications between companies and their shareholders by enacting a number of amendments about blogs, proxies, and electronic shareholder forums. The electronic communication tools allow companies to gain valuable information about their investors and solicit feedback, but they also demand somebody who is very savvy in public relations as the access to information and the speed of communications increase exponentially. It won't take long before investor relations officers will face negative and even obnoxious postings in their electronic communication channels—visible to everybody and sometimes coming at the worst possible time. How prepared will investor relations officers be to deal with this fast-paced and 24/7 communication challenge?

Prepared or unprepared, social media is constantly evolving thus demanding investor relations officers to update their training and evolve with the technology. In addition, investor relations departments should take the lead in developing social media communications with the financial markets. This requires good public relations skills and good understanding of the nature of social media. Although today some see social media as a "large microphone for pushing out information,"[2] such approach is not sustained in the social media landscape. Social media is a tool for dialogue and using it for pushing out information can cause more harm than good as the audiences will resist the push, challenge the information, and provide critical feedback.

Social media is perhaps a better monitoring and diagnostic tool rather than a microphone as it enables the company to constantly scan shareholder forums, blogs, and microblogs for the issues relevant to the corporation and identify such issues early before they grow beyond repair and spill over to newspapers, TV news, and the professional investment community.

Social media can also allow the scope of the dialogue between the corporation and its shareholders to expand. As noted earlier, investors are increasingly concerned with issues of environmental sustainability, fair treatment of employees, and social accountability. Although these issues do not always make it into traditional corporate disclosures, companies are using other channels to communicate their commitment to corporate social responsibility. The amount of companies producing stand-alone corporate social responsibility reports is growing. Yet since there are no standards in accounting for corporate social responsibility, social media enables companies to explain and discuss their actions in this arena as well as listen to the concerns from the interested audiences from around the globe.

Indeed, the globalization of the investment markets is at its highest point. In fact, investment globalization from largely one-directional phenomena becomes truly global. Just 10 years ago, companies from all over the world could not envision a better outcome than listing on New York Stock Exchange (NYSE). The programs of American Depositary Receipts that allowed foreign issuers easy access to U.S. capital markets were flourishing.

Today, however, investment market looks more like a two-way street. U.S. companies are now also looking for foreign investors. A U.S. company may choose to conduct initial public offering of securities in Europe or list their securities on London Stock Exchange instead of NYSE or NASDAQ. Even the companies trading domestically on NYSE or NAS-DAQ have increasing amount of shareholders from all over the world. Now combine it with electronic shareholder forums and XBRL. An investor in Asia will wake up to a fresh data set received through the XBRL-enabled channel and posts something erroneous at company's electronic forum at 1 a.m. EST. By the time an investor relations officer has a chance to react, half of the world read that posting on the company's own investor relations forum, no matter how offensive, negative, or erroneous that comment might have been. Too much moderation or premoderation won't solve the problem either—Dell learned it the hard way when the discussions of Dell's customer service moved from Dell's official site to an independent blog. Shareholders could also find their ways of communicating to each other independent of the corporate oversight—across the world and instantaneously.

This calls for even more proactive shareholder research. It would become truly important to know owners of company stocks and the way they would react to company and market events. Yet more and more shares today are owned in the name of various brokers: "Most shares in public companies (roughly 85 percent) are held in 'street name'—legally owned by brokers on behalf of their customers, the beneficial owners."[3] As a result, companies often do not even know who the real owners of their stock are. To know the shareholders, investor relations officers will need to acquire information on the real beneficial owners of their stock.

The SEC considers several measures to help investor relations officers learn about the company's true shareholders. One of such proposals actively discussed now is Shareholder Communication Coalition Plan. This proposal, if adopted, will allow corporate investor relations officers to move beyond nominal holders of their securities to indentify the actual beneficial owners of stock and to establish direct streams of two-way communication with them. Needless to say, the beneficial investors will be located all over the globe and require more international efforts on behalf of the company and its investor relations officers.

Corporations' global commitment will increase even more as a result. Today, Pfizer CEO Jeff Kinder organized a teleconference at 2 a.m. EST. The timing of the teleconference, seemingly inappropriate just a few years ago, allowed Kinder to communicate with Pfizer and Wyeth employees in Australia and Asia more effectively. Showing employees of remote branches the dedication of corporate headquarters is essential for a global company to operate successfully. There is no doubt that companies of tomorrow will be required to teleconference at 2 a.m. EST with investors and analysts from the remote locations as well, as such locations produce more and more investors daily.

Today, financial analysts, investors, and investor relations officers face a problem of different accounting standards as they enter global financial markets. American financial market participants used to U.S. GAAP (generally accepted accounting principles) might have to reevaluate adoption of international financial accounting standards. Significant differences exist between international and U.S. standards, and the costs of conversion or reporting in both standards may be quite high. Yet access to an international investment market may require American corporations to implement the change. In addition, government and nongovernment agencies are also considering changes to U.S. GAAP itself including making it more compatible with international accounting standards.

Certainly, the future of investor relations will require the profession to change to meet the demands of tomorrow. It is, however, unlikely that the main goals of the profession will change. The investor relations professionals will still be required to build mutually beneficial relationships between corporations and their shareholders based on open, two-way communications.

About the Author

Alexander V. Laskin is an assistant professor at the Department of Public Relations, Quinnipiac University. He received a degree in economic geography and English (1998) from Moscow State Pedagogical University; MA in communication studies (2003) from the University of Northern Iowa; MA in international business (2008) from the University of Florida; and PhD in mass communication (2008) from the University of Florida.

Professor Laskin has extensive work experience in investor relations, international mergers and acquisitions, marketing research, and public relations.

Today, Professor Laskin's academic research focuses on investor relations, strategic corporate communications, social responsibility, and international business. His research was published in leading academic journals such as *Journal of Business Communication, Journal of Communication Management*, and *Public Relations Review*. Professor Laskin's research on the value of investor relations was recognized by the Institute for Public Relations with 2006 Ketchum Excellence in Public Relations Research Award. Professor Laskin is a member of National Investor Relations Institute, Public Relations Society of America, and Association for Business Communication.

Notes

Chapter 2

1. NIRI Board (2003).
2. Thompson (2002), p. 1.
3. Cogner (2004), p. 3.
4. Marcus and Wallace (1997), p. 13.

Chapter 3

1. Morrill (1995).
2. Silver (2004), p. 70.
3. Morrill (1995), chap. 1.
4. Morrill (1995), chap. 1.
5. Robinson (1966), p. 40.
6. Morrill (1995), chap. 1.
7. Morrill (1995), chap. 1.
8. Laskin (2006).
9. Morrill (1995), chap. 1.
10. Chatlos (1984), p. 85.
11. Cutlip, Center, and Broom (2000), p. 107.
12. Morrill (1995), chap. 2.
13. Morrill (1995), chap. 2.
14. Chatlos (1984), p. 87.
15. Morrill (1995), chap. 1.
16. Chatlos (1984), p. 87.
17. Higgins (2000), p. 24
18. Morrill (1995) chap. 1.
19. Chatlos (1984), p. 88.
20. Higgins (2000), pp. 24–25.
21. Marcus and Wallace (1997), p. xi.
22. Ryan and Jacobs (2005), p. 69.

Chapter 4

1. Laskin (2009).
2. Allen (2002).
3. Laskin (2008).
4. Favaro (2001), p. 7.
5. Budd (1993), pp. 44–45.
6. Allen (2002), p. 211.
7. Favaro (2001), p. 7.
8. Silver (2004), p. 60.
9. Savage (1973), pp. 126–127.
10. Grunig (1984).
11. Murphy (1991).
12. Allen (2002), p. 209.
13. Rao and Sivakumar (1999), p. 30
14. Laskin (2009).
15. Martin (2007), p. 191.
16. Kelly, Laskin, and Rosenstein (in press).
17. Tuominen (1997), p. 46.
18. Wiesel, Skiera, and Villanueva (2008), p. 1.
19. Hockerts and Moir (2004), p. 85.

Chapter 5

1. Securities and Exchange Commission (n.d.).
2. Securities and Exchange Commission (2000).
3. Bloxham and Nash (2007), p. 14.
4. Allen (2002), p. 206.
5. A Guide to the Sarbanes-Oxley (2003).

Chapter 6

1. Rao and Sivakumar (1999), p. 27.
2. Yoshikawa (2002).
3. Sharp (2006), p. 2.
4. Aaron (2009), p. 10.
5. Wolff-Reid (2009).

Chapter 7

1. Laskin (2009).
2. Laskin (2009).
3. Rao and Sivakumar (1999), p. 30.
4. Laskin (2009).
5. Laskin (2009).
6. Thompson (2002).

Chapter 8

1. Laskin (2006).
2. As cited in Plitch (2006), p. 1
3. Laskin (2007), p. 23.
4. Ayres and Cramton (1994).
5. Mahoney (2001), pp. 9–10.
6. Bhagat, Black, and Blair (2004), p. 8.
7. See, for example, Eyuboglu and Buja (2007); Levitt (1981; 1983)
8. Dobrzynsky (1993), p. 68.
9. Dobrzynsky (1993), p. 68.
10. Dobrzynsky (1993), p. 68.
11. Dobrzynsky (1993).
12. Bhagat, Black, and Blair (2004), p. 5.
13. Roe (1994).
14. Burke (2005).
15. Walker and Marr (2001).
16. Black (1990).
17. The high level group (2002), p. 48

Chapter 9

1. Wallan (2003), p. v.
2. Hand and Lev (2003), p. 1.
3. Lev (2004), p. 109.
4. Lev (2005), p. 299.
5. Ernst & Young (1997).
6. Marcus and Wallace (1997), p. 14.
7. Hand and Lev (2003), p. 1.
8. Light (1998), p. 17.
9. Ittner and Larcker (2000), p. 2.
10. Lev (2004), p. 109.
11. Lev (2004), p. 111.

12. Lev (2004), p. 110.

13. Amir, Lev, and Sougiannis (2003), p. 1.

14. Hand and Lev (2003), p. 2.

15. Lev, Nissim, and Thomas (2002).

16. Lev (2004), p. 110.

17. Lev (2004), p. 112.

18. Gelb and Siegel (2000), p. 207.

19. Pangarkar and Kirkwood (2006), p. 102.

20. Kaplan and Norton (1996b), p. 71.

21. Pangarkar and Kirkwood (2006), p. 2.

Chapter 10

1. See, for example, Pangarkar and Kirkwood (2006); Ittner and Larcker (2000).

2. Interbrand (2007; 2006; 2005).

3. Amir, Lev, and Sougiannis (2003).

4. Nakamura (2003).

5. Bushell (2004).

6. Lev (2001).

7. Lev (2005).

8. Lev (2004).

9. Amir, Lev, and Sougiannis (1996); Deng, Lev, and Narin (2003).

10. Aboody and Lev (2000).

11. Lev (2002).

12. Lev (2001), p. 5.

13. Greenspan (2002).

14. Lev (2005).

15. Lev (2005), p. 300.

16. Lazear (2000).

17. Lev (2005).

18. Lev (2001), p. 7.

19. Calabro (2001).

20. Ittner and Larcker (1998).

21. Norreklit (2003).

22. Kaplan and Norton (1992; 1993).

23. Kaplan and Norton (1996a; 1996b).

24. Kaplan and Norton (2000; 2001; 2004; 2006).

25. Calabro (2001).

26. Hendricks, Menor, and Wiedman (2004), p. 1.

27. Bessire and Baker (2005).

28. Bontis, Dragonetti, Jacobsen, and Roos (1999).

29. Hendricks, Menor, and Wiedman (2004).
30. Kaplan and Norton (1992), p. 73.
31. Kaplan and Norton (1992).
32. Kaplan and Norton (1992), p. 76.
33. Kaplan and Norton (1996), p. viii.
34. Ernst & Young (1997), p. 1.
35. Ernst & Young (1997), p. 6.
36. Ernst & Young (1997), pp. 8–9.
37. Ernst & Young (1997), pp. 13–14.

Chapter 11

1. Morgan (2009).
2. Morgan (2009), p. 1.
3. Yurow (2009), p. 13.

References

A guide to the Sarbanes-Oxley. (2003). *Summary of section 302*. Retrieved January 1, 2010, from http://www.soxlaw.com/s302.htm

Aaron, M. (2009, November). The long reach of NIRI. *IR Update*, p. 10.

Aboody, D., & Lev, B. (2000). Information asymmetry R&D and insider gains. *The Journal of Finance, 55*(6), 2747–2766.

Allen, C. E. (2002). Building mountains in a flat landscape: Investor relations in the post-Enron era. *Corporate Communications: An International Journal, 7*(4), 206–211.

Amir, E., Lev, B., & Sougiannis, T. (2003). Do financial analysts get intangibles? *European Accounting Review, 12*(4), 635–659.

Ayres, I., & Cramton, P. (1994). Relational investing and agency theory. *Cardozo Law Review, 15*(1033), 1–18.

Bessire, D., & Baker, R. (2005). The French tableau de bord and the American balanced scorecard: A critical analysis. *Critical Perspectives on Accounting, 16*(6), 645–664.

Bhagat, S., Black, B., & Blair, M. (2004). Relational investing and firm performance. *Journal of Financial Research, 27*(1), 1–30.

Black, B. (1990). Shareholder passivity reexamined. *Michigan Law Review, 89*, 520–608.

Bloxham, E., & Nash, J. (2007, December). SOX: Why it happened and why it has been good for investors and companies—The child grows up! *Investor Relations Update*, pp. 14–15.

Bontis, N., Dragonetti, N., Jacobsen, K., & Roos, G. (1999). The knowledge toolbox: A review of the tools available to measure and manage intangible resources. *European Management Journal, 17*(4), 391–402.

Budd, J. F. (1993). *CEO credibility: The management of reputation*. Lakeville, CT: Turtle Publishing Company.

Burke, E. M. (2005). *Managing a company in an activist world: The leadership challenge of corporate citizenship*. London, United Kingdom: Praeger Publishers.

Bushell, S. (2004, October 6). From zero to one hundred. *CIO*. Retrieved January 1, 2010, from CIO website: http://www.cio.com.au/index.php/id;598455995

Calabro, L. (2001, February). On balance. *CFO Magazine*. Retrieved January 1, 2010, from CFO Publishing website: http://www.cfo.com/printable/article.cfm/2991608

Chatlos, W. E. (1984). Investor relations. In B. Cantor (Ed.), *Experts in action: Inside public relations* (pp. 84–101). New York, NY: Longman.

Conger, M. (2004, January/February). How a comprehensive IR program pays off. *Financial Executive 1*, pp. 1–4. Retrieved January 1, 2010, from Financial Executive International website: http://www.fei.org

Cutlip, S. M., Center, A. H., & Broom, G. M. (2000). *Effective public relations* (8th ed.). Upper Saddle River, NJ: Prentice Hall.

Deng, Z., Lev, B., & Narin, F. (2003). Science and technology as predictors of stock performance. In R. M. Hand & B. Lev (Eds.), *Intangible assets: Values, measures, and risks* (pp. 207–227). New York, NY: Oxford University Press.

Dobrzynsky, J. H. (1993, March 15). Relationship investing. *BusinessWeek 3309*, 68.

Ernst & Young (1997). *Measures than matter*. Boston, MA: Ernst & Young Center for Business Innovation.

Eyuboglu, N., & Buja, A. (2007). Quasi-Darwinian selection in marketing relationships. *Journal of Marketing, 71*(4), 48–62.

Favaro, P. (2001). Beyond bean counting: The CFO's expanding role. *Strategy & Leadership, 29*(5), 4–8.

Gelb, D. S., & Siegel, P. (2000). Intangible assets and corporate signaling. *Review of Quantitative Finance and Accounting, 15*(4), 307–323.

Greenspan, A. (2002, February 27). *Testimony of Chairman Alan Greenspan: Federal Reserve Board's semiannual monetary policy report to the Congress.* Retrieved January 1, 2010, from Federal Reserve Board website: http://www.federalreserve.gov/boarddocs/hh/2002/february/testimony.htm

Grunig, J. E. (1984). Organizations, environments, and models of public relations. *Public Relations Research & Education, 1*(1), 6–29.

Hand, R. M., & Lev, B. (2003). *Intangible assets: Values, measures, and risks.* New York, NY: Oxford University Press.

Hendricks, K. B., Menor, L., & Wiedman, C. (2004). The balanced scorecard: To adopt or not to adopt? *Ivey Business Journal, 69*(2), 1–9.

The high level group of company law experts. (2002). *Report of the high level group of company law experts on a modern regulatory framework for company law in Europe.* Brussels: European Commission. Retrieved January 1, 2010, from European Commission website: http://ec.europa.eu/internal_market/company/docs/modern/report_en.pdf

Higgins, R. B. (2000). *Best practices in global investor relations: The creation of shareholder value.* Westport, CT: Quorum Books.

Hockerts, K., & Moir, L. (2004). Communicating corporate responsibility to investors: The changing role of the investor relations function. *Journal of Business Ethics, 52*(1), 85–98.

Interbrand. (2005). *Best global brands 2005.* Retrieved January 1, 2010, from Interbrand website: http://www.interbrand.com

Interbrand. (2006). *Best global brands 2006.* Retrieved January 1, 2010, from Interbrand website: http://www.interbrand.com/

Interbrand. (2007). *Best global brands 2007.* Retrieved January 1, 2010, from Interbrand website: http://www.interbrand.com/

Ittner, C. D., & Larcker, D. F. (1998). Innovations in performance measurement: Trends and research implications. *Journal of Management Accounting Research, 10,* 205–238.

Kaplan, R. S., & Norton, D. P. (1992). The balanced scorecard: Measures that drive performance. *Harvard Business Review, 70*(1), 71–79.

Kaplan, R. S., & Norton, D. P. (1993). Putting the balanced scorecard to work. *Harvard Business Review, 71*(5), 134–142.

Kaplan, R. S., & Norton, D. P. (1996a). Using the balanced scorecard as a management system. *Harvard Business Review, 74*(1), 75–85.

Kaplan, R. S., & Norton, D. P. (1996b). *The balanced scorecard: Translating strategy into action.* Boston, MA: Harvard Business School Press.

Kaplan, R. S., & Norton, D. P. (2000). Having trouble with your strategy? Then map it. *Harvard Business Review, 78*(5), 167–176.

Kaplan, R. S., & Norton, D. P. (2001). The strategy-focused organization: How balanced scorecard companies thrive in new business environment. Boston, MA: Harvard Business School Press.

Kaplan, R. S., & Norton, D. P. (2004). *Strategy maps: Converting intangible assets into tangible outcomes.* Boston, MA: Harvard Business School Press.

Kaplan, R. S., & Norton, D. P. (2006). *Alignment: Using the balanced scorecard to create corporate synergies.* Boston, MA: Harvard Business School Press.

Kelly, K. S., Laskin, A. V., & Rosenstein, G. A. (in press). Investor relations: Two-way symmetrical practice. *Journal of Public Relations Research.*

Laskin, A. V. (2006). Investor relations practices at Fortune-500 companies: An exploratory study. *Public Relations Review, 32*(1), 69–70.

Laskin, A. V. (2007). *The value of investor relations: A Delphi panel investigation.* Gainesville, FL: The Institute for Public Relations. Retrieved January 1, 2010, from The Institute for Public Relations website: http://www .instituteforpr.org/

Laskin, A. V. (2008, November). *Essential knowledge project: Investor relations.* Gainesville, FL: Institute for Public Relations. Retrieved January 1, 2010, from The Institute for Public Relations website: http://www.instituteforpr .org/

Laskin, A. V. (2009). A descriptive account of the investor relations profession: A national study. *Journal of Business Communication, 46*(2), 208–233.

Lazear, E. (2000). Performance pay and productivity. *American Economic Review, 90*(3), 1346–1361.

Lev, B. (2001). *Intangibles.* Washington, DC: The Brookings Institution Press.

Lev, B. (2002).Where have all of Enron's intangibles gone? *Journal of Accounting and Public Policy, 21,* 131–135.

Lev, B. (2003). What then must we do? In R. M. Hand & B. Lev (Eds.), *Intangible assets: Values, measures, and risks* (pp. 511–524). New York, NY: Oxford University Press.

Lev, B. (2004). Sharpening the intangibles edge. *Harvard Business Review, 82*(6), 109–116.

Lev, B. (2005). Intangible assets: Concepts and measurements. *Encyclopedia of Social Measurement, 2,* 299–305.

Lev, B., Nissim, D., & Thomas, J. (2002). *On the informational usefulness of R&D capitalization and amortization.* Working paper. New York, NY: Columbia University, School of Business.

Lev, B., & Sougiannis, T. (1996). The capitalization, amortization, and value-relevance of R&D. *Journal of Accounting and Economics, 21*(1), 107–138.

Levitt, T. (1981). Marketing intangible products and product intangibles. *Harvard Business Review, 59*(3), 94–102.

Levitt, T. (1983). After the sale is over. . . . *Harvard Business Review, 61*(5), 87–93.

Light, D. A. (1998). Performance measurement. *Harvard Business Review, 76*(6), 17–20.

Mahoney, W. F. (2001). *The strategy and practice of investor relations.* New York, NY: The NASDAQ Stock Market, Inc.

Marcus, B. W., & Wallace, S. L. (1997). *New dimensions in investor relations: Competing for capital in the 21st century.* Hoboken, NJ: John Wiley & Sons.

Martin, E. F., Jr. (2007). Using wave theory to maximize retail investor media communications. *International Journal of Strategic Communication, 1*(3), 191–206.

Morgan, J. (2009, November 3). President's Note. *IR Weekly,* 1–2.

Morgan, J. (2009, December 8). President's Note. *IR Weekly,* 1–2.

Morrill, D. C. (1995). *Origins of NIRI.* Vienna, VA: The National Investor Relations Institute. Retrieved March 1, 2007, from The National Investor Relations Institute website: http://www.niri.org/about/origins.cfm

Murphy, P. (1991). The limits of symmetry: A game theory approach to symmetric and asymmetrical public relations. *Public Relations Research Annual, 3,* 115–131.

Nakamura, L. (2003). A trillion dollars a year in intangible investment and the new economy. In R. M. Hand & B. Lev (Eds.), *Intangible assets: Values, measures, and risks* (pp. 19–47). New York, NY: Oxford University Press.

NIRI Board of Directors. (2003, March). *Mission and goals.* Retrieved January 1, 2010, from NIRI website: http://www.niri.org/about/mission.cfm

Norreklit, H. (2003). The balanced scorecard: What is the score? A rhetorical analysis of the balanced scorecard. *Accounting, Organizations and Society* 28(6), 591–619.

Pangarkar, A. M., & Kirkwood, T. (2006). *Strategic alignment new accountabilities: Non-financial measures of performance.* Chicago, IL: MediaTec Publishing.

Plitch, P. (2006, April 6). More US companies take Google-esque approach to guidance. *Dow Jones News Service.*

Rao, H., & Sivakumar, K. (1999). Institutional sources of boundary-spanning structures: The establishment of investor relations departments in the Fortune 500 industrials. *Organizational Science, 10*(1), 27–42.

Robinson, E. J. (1966). *Communication and public relations.* Columbus, OH: Charles E. Merrill.

Roe, M. J. (1994). *Strong managers, weak owners: The political roots of American corporate finance.* Princeton, NJ: Princeton University Press.

Ryan, T. M., & Jacobs, C. A. (2005). *Using investor relations to maximize equity valuation.* Hoboken, NJ: Wiley Finance.

Securities and Exchange Commission. (n.d.). *The investors advocate: How the SEC protects investors, maintains market integrity, and facilitates capital formation.* Retrieved January 1, 2010, from SEC website: http://www.sec.gov/about/whatwedo.shtml

Securities and Exchange Commission. (2000). *Final rule: Selective disclosure and insider trading.* Retrieved January 1, 2010, from SEC website: http://www.sec.gov/rules/final/33-7881.htm

Sharp, D. J. (2006*). Cases in business ethics.* Thousand Oaks, CA: Sage.

Silver, D. (2004). The IR-PR nexus. In B. M. Cole (Ed.), *The new investor relations: Experts perspective on the state of the art* (pp. 59–88). Princeton, NJ: Bloomberg Press.

Thompson, L. M. (2002, April 9). NIRI ten points program to help restore investor confidence. *NIRI's Executive Alert.* Retrieved January 1, 2010, from NIRI website: http://www.niri.org/irresource_pubs/alerts/ea040902.pdf

Tuominen, P. (1997). Investor relations: A Nordic school approach. *Corporate Communications, 2*(1), 46–55.

Walker, S. F., & Marr, J. W. (2001). *Stakeholder power: A winning strategy for building stakeholder commitment and driving corporate growth.* Cambridge, MA: Perseus Publishing.

Wallman, S. (2003). Foreword. In R. M. Hand & B. Lev (Eds.), *Intangible assets: Values, measures, and risks* (pp. v–vi) New York, NY: Oxford University Press.

Wiesel, T., Skiera, B., & Villanueva, J. (2008). Customer equity: An integral part of financial reporting. *Journal of Marketing, 72*(2), 1–14.

Wolff-Reid, M. (2009, August). Meeting challenges in 2009 capital markets. *IR Update, 8*, 9–11.

Yoshikawa, T., & Gedajlovic, E. (2002). The impact of global capital market exposure and stable ownership on investor relations practices and performance of Japanese firms. *Asia Pacific Journal of Management, 19*, 525–540.

Yurow, L. (2009). NYSE's rule 452 in a nutshell. *IR Update, 9*, 13–14.

Index